D0834501

Run Smart

Training Tips for Runners

Adam Hodges

Alp Multisport Publications

Born in the Rocky Mountains of Colorado

alpmultisport.com

Visit the Alp Multisport website for video demos of drills
and exercises discussed in this book. Run smart!

Additional titles from Alp Multisport Publications:

The Endurance Athlete's Guide
Adam Hodges

Multisport Workout Library
Adam Hodges

Copyright © 2013 Adam Hodges

All rights reserved.

Print Edition

ISBN: 0988609541
ISBN-13: 978-0-9886095-4-9

DEDICATION

For the love of running

We shall not cease from exploration
And the end of all our exploring
Will be to arrive where we started
And know the place for the first time.

~ T.S. Eliot

CONTENTS

ADAM HODGES

PREFACE

Running has been an integral part of my life since I first got involved in the sport around age 10. Not only has it contributed to my health and well-being over the intervening decades, it has allowed me to meet fabulous people, explore amazing terrain, and visit beautiful places around the world. Nothing is more rewarding, in my mind, than traveling over rugged trails on my own two feet. And there is much to be said for the pure simplicity of running, along with the opportunities it affords all of us as a vehicle for discovery, adventure, and obtaining a glimpse of human potential.

This book contains a selection of articles I have written as a coach for runners looking to get involved in the sport or take their running to the next level. Since each chapter consists of a self-contained article, the book is intended to be picked up and read more like a magazine or act like a reference guide to various dimensions of the sport. Readers that choose to skip around, moving across different parts of the book to read an article here or there, will therefore gain as much as readers who choose to read the book in a more traditional manner. The chapters are arranged by topic and represent a general progression through a range of issues that include goal setting, mental skills, training principles, warmup protocols, running drills, functional strength, running form, running shoes, nutrition, hydration, recovery, and sleep.

There are obviously many details that factor into a runner's success, from anatomy to physiology to biomechanics to psychology to nutrition. Whether one competes in races or runs for personal health and fitness, learning more about the ins-and-outs of running is an important step toward becoming a better, faster, and more efficient runner—ultimately enabling one to squeeze more enjoyment and longevity out of the sport. But underlying it all, the simplicity of running remains. In the end, when we head out that door, we still just run. And there is nothing like experiencing the simplicity of a run—to run for the pure love of running. So enjoy the running lifestyle, and along the way, run smart!

WHY RUN?

You have to wonder at times what you're doing out there. Over the years, I've given myself a thousand reasons to keep running, but it always comes back to where it started. It comes down to self-satisfaction and a sense of achievement.

~Steve Prefontaine

Why run? As American distance runner Steve Prefontaine taught us, the real purpose of running is to test the limits of the human heart. And we should take this to mean both physically and metaphorically.

Running is about testing personal limits, and competitors in races aid us in this endeavor. We strive to reach new personal bests, and we achieve satisfaction knowing we put forth the best effort that we can…with what we've got…on any given race day.

And ultimately, giving your best is what running and racing is all about, whether you reach the podium, set a personal record, or simply do what you can at the moment (even if you're zapped by the remnants of a cold). We run, we gain experience, and we learn from that experience.

To give anything less than your best is to sacrifice the gift.

~Steve Prefontaine

BEGIN IT NOW

Whatever you can do, or dream you can do, begin it. Boldness has genius, power, and magic in it. Begin it now.

These lines, often attributed to Goethe, seem particularly appropriate at the start of any new training program.

If you have had your sights set on a dream you have never quite been able to act upon, heed the call. Begin it. Begin it now.

Here are three key steps to help you put flesh on that ambition.

Set a Goal

Put your goal down in writing, using the SMART mnemonic as a guide. This is the first step to making your dream a reality. Namely, goals should be specific, measurable, challenging yet realistically attainable, relevant to the current point and time of your life, and time-bound. 有时限的 Then share the goal with others, and enlist their support.

Create a Plan

Once you have given your goal some materiality by writing it down, next you need to create a concrete plan to take you from here to there.

Monitor Your Progress and Adjust Your Course

A goal and a plan require monitoring to keep you on the right path. Keep track of your training. Periodically schedule benchmark workouts to test your fitness and assess your progress. Use feedback along the way to make adjustments as needed to stay on target. Keep in mind that the path from a goal's inception to fruition is rarely a straight, smooth line.

Four Simple Ways to Become a Better Runner

As you plan your training strategy for those goals on your list, here are four healthy habits to add to that strategy. Working these positive practices into your life will help you become a better runner.

① Add Functional Strength Work to Your Training

The principle of specificity states that runners must spend the majority of their training time dedicated to running. Yet spending all your training time in this pursuit is a recipe for overuse injuries. To be sure, any runner will benefit greatly from supplemental strength training that focuses on functional exercises.

Time-crunched athletes need only dedicate an extra ten minutes three to six days per week to become stronger and less injury prone. You can incorporate a ten minute sequence into your daily activities without the need to go to a gym. For example, set aside ten minutes upon waking in the morning, ten minutes while taking a break from work in the afternoon, or ten minutes while watching your favorite television show in the evening.

Learn to Run with a Quicker Cadence

The path towards becoming a more efficient runner begins with baby steps—that is, quick baby steps. As you begin your base training for the season ahead, focus on developing a quick cadence that targets 84-90 foot strikes per minute. That corresponds to 28-30 foot strikes per 20 seconds, or 42-45 per 30 seconds. A "foot strike" refers to a single foot—left or right.

Not only will you increase your running efficiency, but a quicker cadence helps spread out the impact forces associated with running to help alleviate some of the stress on your joints.

Running over hot coals with quick steps is a good visual image to put in your mind, along with the tick-tock sound of a metronome set at the right frequency.

Incorporate Drills into Your Easy Workouts

Good form equals free speed, and the key to developing good form is to ingrain proper movement patterns into your muscle memory so that it becomes automatic even when fatigue threatens to break it down.

To develop good form, incorporate supplemental form drills into your training. Easy workout days are especially good opportunities to focus on form.

Use Short-term and Long-term Goals to Guide You to Desired Results

What do you want to accomplish this season and in the years ahead? What abilities do you want to improve? What are your top priority races and what do you want to accomplish at these races?

Writing down your goals and assessing your progress can be a powerful means for achieving great things.

Ten Guidelines for Effective Goal Setting

The longest journey begins with a single step.

~Lao Tzu

When properly implemented, goal setting can play a key role in helping an athlete achieve desired results. Here are ten guidelines to help you use goal setting more effectively.

Set Long-term, Intermediate, and Short-term Goals

Think of the goal setting process like climbing a mountain. Your ultimate goal may be the summit (long-term goal); but to reach the summit, you need to break the climb into segments (intermediate goals) and divide those segments into individual steps (short-term goals).

Keep Records and Evaluate Progress

Write down your goals, and schedule dates for their evaluation. Feedback is an essential component of the goal setting process. The feedback you gain along the way will allow you to readjust your short-term and intermediate goals to stay on course for the long-term ones.

Set Goals for Both Training and Racing

Goals are not just for races. It is equally important to include goals in your training. Benchmark goals can help you monitor your progress on a regular basis, and daily or weekly training goals can help you stay focused on the training objectives of the moment.

Set Goals That Are Difficult yet Realistic

Goals should be challenging. After all, if you can easily do something, there's little need to make it a goal. Yet goals also need to be grounded in reality. Goals too far removed from an honest assessment of one's abilities can be discouraging in the long run. Goals should keep you motivated. They should challenge you to step up to that next level of performance. You may not always reach a particular goal, but that's part of the process. It's better to reach high and progress than to aim low and never really test your capabilities.

Devise Goals That Are Specific

Specific goals, rather than vague ones, will provide precision to your training program. Instead of saying, "I want to improve my marathon time" (vague), specify, "I want to qualify for the Boston Marathon next year" (specific).

Devise Goals That Are Measurable

Devising goals that are specific goes hand in hand with devising goals that are measurable. If you want to qualify for the Boston Marathon, for example, that can be measured—namely, you can compare your race times to the qualifying times. Measurable goals often involve time targets, e.g. "I want to run a sub-3:40 marathon."

State Goals in the Positive

Keep your eyes focused on where you want to go rather than where you don't want to go. Instead of saying, "I don't want to run slower than 40 minutes in the Memorial Day 10K" (negative), state, "I want to break 40 minutes for the Memorial Day 10K" (positive).

Keep Goals under Your Control

As much as possible, set goals that you have control over. This means focusing more on performance and process goals than outcome goals.

Performance goals have to do with achieving a certain time (e.g. breaking 10 hours in the Ironman, running a 40 minute 10K).

Process goals have to do with how you compete (e.g. keep my cadence high during the last half of the run).

Outcome goals have to do with placement in a race (e.g. finishing on the podium).

While outcome goals provide long-term motivation and many long-term goals take this form, performance and process goals help us focus on what we need to do in the intermediate and short-term, such as in the moment of the race.

Own Your Goals

Devise and write down goals that are agreeable to you, that you will commit to, and that you are willing to accept as your own. After all, these are your goals and should represent what you want to achieve, not what you think others want you to accomplish.

Involve a Support System

Let supporters (e.g. friends, family, training partners) know what your goals are so that they can help you stay accountable to those goals and provide encouragement along the way.

KEEPING YOUR HEAD IN THE GAME

There's nothing either good or bad but thinking makes it so.

~Shakespeare

Given that optimal performance relies as much on psychology as physiology, the best physical preparation in the world can only take an athlete so far. As anyone who has ever engaged in a performance activity knows, the situation can induce a significant level of mental stress in addition to the physical stress placed on the body. So how can we minimize that mental stress to best support performance?

The key is to first recognize that *our thinking guides how we feel and what we do*. It's a simple aphorism, but it often gets lost amidst the chaos of race morning. When we approach a performance activity, such as an A-level race, the beliefs we have as we approach the event substantially impact how we will respond once the racing gets underway.

Thoughts can sabotage performance or thoughts can enhance performance. Obviously, thoughts that hinder performance are to be avoided while those that facilitate performance should be developed. With this in mind, I have broken down the cognitive techniques needed to support optimal performance into two corresponding phases for mental skills training.

Mental Training Phase 1
Developing Self-Awareness

Zen masters have long pointed out that our minds are filled with busy chatter. For the athlete, the first step in mental training is to recognize the thoughts that comprise that chatter. What thoughts typically go through your mind while running those track intervals? When you pack your transition bag the day before a race? When you wake up on the morning of race day? When you step to the starting line? Pay attention to your thoughts on a daily basis with particular attention to the moments before, during and after your physical training.

Once you've developed greater awareness of the thoughts that occupy your mind, learn to identify irrational thoughts. Irrational thoughts stem from beliefs such as perfectionism, which holds that one must always perform well, or the belief that conditions in life should be arranged so that we get what we want quickly, easily and comfortably. Such beliefs lead to anxiety and mental stress. They also form the basis of irrational thoughts, which commonly occur in forms that focus on (i) the awful, terrible or horrible (e.g. *It's so awful that my chain broke; How horrible that I dropped my water bottle*), (ii) the unbearable (e.g. *I can't stand the heat; Waiting in this line is unbearable*), (iii) worthlessness (e.g. *I'm a lousy runner; My stride is awful*), or (iv) overgeneralizations and exaggerations (e.g. *I always; I never*).

In addition to negative thoughts that are self-deprecating or self-punishing, other thoughts that work against an athlete's ability to perform optimally consist of irrelevant, disrupting or distracting thoughts. If you are in the middle of an interval session and your mind is focused on composing your shopping list, it will be difficult to properly attend to the training task at hand.

In contrast, we want to develop cognitive habits that inculcate positive thoughts that enhance self-worth, confidence, and energy levels, along with positive directives that facilitate performance by focusing attention on task-relevant actions. This takes us to the second phase of mental training.

Mental Training Phase 2
Developing Positive Cognitive Habits

Once we have learned to recognize irrational and negative thoughts, we can then take proactive steps to overcome them. Counter irrational thoughts with rational thinking; and learn to stop negative thoughts by replacing them with positive ones. This can be achieved through the use of mental jujutsu whereby the mind identifies a negative thought and then turns it on its head so that its positive correlate becomes the focus of attention instead. In this way, negative thoughts that focus on, say, deficits can be turned into positive thoughts that focus on skills and abilities.

For example, maybe you're worried about your speed going into a race due to an injury that caused you to start speed work later than expected in your training. If you find yourself worrying about this deficit on race day, turn your attention instead to the increased aerobic base and general strength you now have because you invested more time on base building and cross-training. Instead of worrying about your finishing kick, think: *I'm a strong runner. I have more running fitness than usual for this point in the season. I want to make use of my aerobic engine.*

If the mind attaches itself to a past event and begins to worry about it, turn your concentration to the present. Likewise, if the mind drifts to a future event or hypothetical consequence, focus on the present. It is impossible to act in the past (which has already happened) or in the future (which has yet to come), so the only actions we can fully control are the ones we are engaged in at the present moment. Use this simple directive as a mantra to focus your mind's attention on the immediate task at hand: *Do what I can do right now.*

On May 1, 2010, Chris Solinsky became the first American to break 27 minutes in the 10,000-meter run. If you watch his performance, especially over the last several laps, he looks like a gazelle floating effortlessly around the track at remarkable speed. Yet a lap before the halfway point of the race, he developed a potentially race-ending side stitch that lasted another six or seven laps. Fortunately, he was as prepared mentally as he was physically for the race. In his mind, he repeated the instructions that his coach, Jerry Schumacher, had told him prior to the race: "If anything comes up, just take it one lap at a time." And that's exactly what he did. He ran one lap at a time, keeping himself in the race until the stitch went away and he opened up a spectacular kick to finish in record time.

The bottom line is that cognition can be trained. Just as your body responds when you stimulate it with physical training, so does your mind when you stimulate it with positive thinking. A proactive approach to mental training will allow you to take control over your cognitive habits.

A key component of this training consists of constructing and implementing positive self-statements. Positive self-statements are best when they're brief (e.g. *I'm a strong runner*), use positive terminology (e.g. *I am; I can; I will; I want to*) while avoiding obligation words (e.g. *I must; I have to; I should*), focus on strengths (e.g. *I handle fatigue well; I get stronger as the race progresses*), focus on possibilities (e.g. *I will extend myself over the last mile; I will perform well*), and direct you (e.g. *I am focusing on form; I run with a quick cadence*).

Just like physical training, mental skills training benefits from consistent practice. Once you've constructed your own self-statements, incorporate them into your physical training as you would any other aspect of your program. Use them in a variety of situations and environments, including routine workouts, low stress situations, race simulations, and full blown competitions. This will train your mind to take control of the thoughts that arise and positively shape them. When you encounter adverse situations in training or racing—and they will occur—then you will have a set of positive self-statements to fall back on, and you will have the ability to construct new ones for the current situation.

A PURPOSE FOR EVERY WORKOUT

This article is not about semantics; it is about how to improve athletic performance through effective race preparation. But I want to start by considering the difference between a *workout* and *training*.

Defined as "a session of vigorous physical exercise," a *workout* is an important element of training. Yet *training*—defined as "a course of exercise...in preparation for a sporting event"— involves more than simply working out. Training involves an end goal that goes beyond a single session. It is a goal driven process that moves an athlete forward as she prepares for a future athletic event.

In other words, one can perform a workout without necessarily training for an event. One can go out and exercise vigorously, work up a sweat, and enjoy the endorphin release. As a result, one may be happier, healthier, and fitter for having done the workout. But the workout may or may not contribute toward a performance goal in a future athletic contest.

And this brings us to the heart of the matter. If you are an endurance athlete training for an event, it is important to consider how each workout contributes to the goal driven process of preparing for your event. If you don't know why you're doing a particular workout or what training effect you're targeting, you may or may not hit the target. As a result, you may or may not be very effective at preparing for that event.

This is where a systematic approach to training can help you train more effectively. By acting according to a fixed plan or system, a systematic approach allows you to prepare for your event with greater precision.

A systematic approach need not be a complicated approach (although it can be). It simply needs to involve a plan that starts with the end goal in mind, and individual workouts (training sessions) that contribute to that overarching plan.

The bottom line is that knowing the why and the reason for each session marks the distinction between training and simply working out. And training with a purpose is the key to successful race preparation.

A WORKOUT DOES NOT
EQUAL TRAINING

In making the distinction between training and working out, I noted that one can perform a workout without necessarily training for an event:

> One can go out and exercise vigorously, work up a sweat, and enjoy the endorphin release. As a result, one may be happier, healthier, and fitter for having done the workout. But the workout may or may not contribute toward a performance goal in a future athletic contest.

This distinction underscores the need to consider how your workouts contribute to the overall training process. A single workout is not sufficient in and of itself. It must be part of a larger program. Each workout must relate to other workouts of similar type as well as workouts of complementary type.

Workouts of similar type are important because it takes five to twelve similar type training sessions to accumulate the full benefits of that type of training. For example, if you are working on raising your lactate threshold, a single workout at threshold pace is necessary but not sufficient to gain the desired physiological adaptation. It needs to be accompanied by additional similar type workouts (e.g. sustained tempo sessions or cruise intervals at threshold pace) to optimally develop your fitness in that area.

Workouts of complementary type are important because if all you do over five to twelve training days is the same type of workout; then you lack the necessary supporting workouts to make that type of training possible and effective. For example, if you only do high intensity workouts every time you go out to train, your program would lack the necessary sessions to help you recover from those workouts and prepare for subsequent ones. Scheduled recovery and low-intensity aerobic work is just as important as scheduled intervals in a training program. For maximal benefit, the different types of workouts need to work together to support of an overriding goal.

The point is to avoid—if you are targeting a

specific racing goal—a mixed bag approach that lacks consistency and integration with your larger goals. With the mixed bag approach, you may choose one training partner's workout one day and another training partner's workout on another day—and those workouts may provide you with vigorous activities that allow you to work up a sweat, gain an endorphin release, etc.—but those workouts may or may not work together like links in a chain to help you achieve your own racing goals. If you are an athlete in training—and not just an athlete that works out—a systematic, goal-driven approach ensures you are moving as directly and effectively as possible towards your racing goals.

AVOID THE DEAD-END TRAINING ZONE

Let's face it. Most athletes understand what it takes to succeed. It's no secret, after all, that to advance your race readiness, you must put in substantial amounts of hard work. Yet don't let this focus on hard work blind you to the crucial role easy days play in any training program.

It is important to distinguish between working hard during key training sessions and working hard during every training session. If there is one pitfall that many highly motivated athletes fall into, it is not respecting this distinction. This leads them into a "dead-end training zone" much to the detriment of their fitness progression.

By a dead-end training zone, I mean a training zone that is neither hard enough to produce a substantial training effect nor easy enough to allow for proper recovery between key workouts. This type of training devolves into that dreaded enemy of time-crunched athletes known as "junk miles" or "wasted workouts."

To avoid the dead-end training zone, it is important to have a purpose for each training session. In addition, one must respect that purpose and adhere to the mantra of *keeping the hard days hard and the easy days easy.*

Keep in mind that fitness gains are achieved by applying an appropriate training stimulus and then backing off so the body can respond with a positive adaptation that leads to enhanced fitness. Around the middle of the twentieth century, Hungarian biologist Hans Selye termed this *stress-response-adaptation process* the general adaptation syndrome (GAS). The GAS along with the *overload principle*—which states that any new training gain requires a greater amount of training stress—form the basic foundation of training programs.

Yet what often gets lost in the application of these principles is the role recovery plays in the GAS. Although hard work in training is a necessary component of improved fitness (per the overload principle), hard work in and of itself is not sufficient. It must be accompanied by adequate recovery so that the body can positively adapt to the training stress by rebuilding stronger than before.

This is easy enough in theory to comprehend, but many ambitious athletes nevertheless fall into that pitfall of going hard every day or turning easy days into competitions with training partners. Even when training solo, it can sometimes be tempting to push the pace a bit on those recovery days when you are feeling good. "Why not?" you might think to yourself, "If I'm feeling good, I might as well push myself a bit since training gains come through hard work."

What often happens, however, is that those easy workouts that morph into not-quite-so-easy workouts end up taking you into a dead-end zone where you are neither going fast enough to achieve a proper overload nor slow enough to allow for adequate recovery before your next hard session. These are the "junk miles" you want to avoid.

At best, you might carry a little extra fatigue into your next hard day. At worst, you might be unable to hit the training target in the next key workout due to inadequate recovery going into it. Instead of achieving the desired training effect to ratchet up your fitness level, you then need to wait until you are better recovered before trying again.

Remember, every workout has a purpose— including the easy days. The best way to ensure you are ready to work hard and get the most out of those key training sessions is to respect the easy workouts by keeping them easy.

AVOID THE DEAD-END TRAINING ZONE, PART II

In my previous discussion, I outlined a common pitfall many motivated athletes fall into. Namely, they fail to take prescribed easy or low intensity workouts seriously, letting those workouts morph into not-so-easy sessions that take them into a counterproductive "dead-end training zone." Here, I sketch out a scenario to illustrate in more specific terms the concept of the dead-end training zone.

As previously defined:

By a dead-end training zone, I mean a training zone that is neither hard enough to produce a substantial training effect nor easy enough to allow for proper recovery between key workouts. This type of training devolves into that dreaded enemy of time-crunched athletes known as "junk miles" or "wasted workouts." To avoid the dead-end training zone, it is important to have a purpose for each training session. In addition, one must respect that purpose and adhere to the mantra of keeping the hard days hard and the easy days easy.

In terms of the training zone system I use with athletes (as detailed in *The Endurance Athlete's Guide*), the dead-end zone frequently manifests itself when athletes turn prescribed workouts in Zones 1-2 into Zone 3 efforts.[1]

Easy or recovery workouts in Zone 1 are designed to aid recovery, loosen you up for key workouts, and add to your training volume. Endurance workouts in Zone 2 contribute to your training volume and target improved aerobic efficiency—namely, the ability to metabolize fat and spare glycogen as a long duration energy source. Work in Zones 1-2 helps build that all-important aerobic base and prepares you for higher intensity workouts at other points in your training plan.

Let's take a look at a specific scenario where an athlete falls into the dead-end zone:

Ronnie the Runner meets up with his training group for a run around the park. He is coming off some hard training days in

ADAM HODGES

preparation for an upcoming race, so on this day his training plan calls for an easy day. Specifically, he aims to target a 30-40 minute run in Zones 1-2.

As Ronnie the Runner starts out on this day's training run with the group, the pace is conversational and his heart rate monitor indicates he is well within his prescribed range.

But at 15 minutes into the run, a few members of the group start pushing the pace. As a result, the whole group speeds up; and Ronnie the Runner, feeling pretty good, decides to match the pace. At the end of the workout, he realizes he did the bulk of the run in Zone 3 instead of his prescribed "easy" run for the day.

The next day, he goes out for his prescribed threshold workout, which calls for cruise intervals in Zone 4. Feeling fatigued, he is unable to match the prescribed pace and ends up doing half of the intervals in Zone 3 before ending the workout to go home early and rest.

In this scenario, Ronnie the Runner falls into the classic pitfall of the dead-end training zone. Neither reaping the benefits of the easier run nor the benefits of the harder workout, he middles along in a dead-end training zone. In this case, he gets stuck in Zone 3 at a pace that is too hard on his easy day and too easy on his hard day.

At best, if Ronnie the Runner learns how to adjust his training to avoid the dead-end zone, this incident will only slow his progress by a few days as he backs up to get in his needed recovery days so he is ready to come back for the intended hard days. At worst, if Ronnie the Runner repeats this scenario on a frequent basis, he will hit a training plateau or dig himself into an overtraining hole.

What could Ronnie the Runner have done differently in the above scenario?

Sure, it would have been better if he had used the group training run as a truly easy day, staying in Zones 1-2. But, there is also another option he could have chosen to avoid the dead-end zone while feeding that day's need for speed.

As the pace quickened, he could have pushed it even harder into Zone 4 and turned the workout into a tempo run closer to threshold pace. If he truly felt good and was in a fresh enough state to handle the pace, this would have provided him with a quality workout. He would then adjust his schedule over the coming days, turning the next day's originally planned threshold workout into an easy session. As a result, the adjustments would have allowed him to stay on track to hit the training objectives for the week.

The take away point from this scenario is that if you are really feeling fresh on those prescribed easy days and feel the need for speed; then go ahead and target a true quality workout. But if you do so and find that pace too demanding; then that's all the more reason to remain in the prescribed lower intensity zones. The bottom line is that you want to avoid drifting into the dead-end training zone.

Remember, effective training requires more than simply training hard. It requires training smart by systematically balancing hard and easy days to attain sought after fitness gains. Respect the integral role that easy days play in your program and you will reap the rewards with faster times down the road.

LEARNING TO DIFFERENTIATE BETWEEN GEARS IN YOUR TRAINING

Raise your hand if you drive in the same gear whether pulling out of your driveway or driving down the freeway?

At this point in my survey, I'm hoping the room is void of raised hands.

Now, raise your hand if you run at one pace day in and day out?

If you answered yes, this article is for you. The aim is to underscore that one of the fundamental training skills you will want to learn is how to differentiate between gears. Just as there is a different time and place for using the different gears in your car, there is a different time and place for using different training speeds. Whether you race against yourself or others, the key to improved performance is learning how to use those different speeds to optimize your training effectiveness.

One-speed runners come in different flavors. For the sake of simplicity, let's sketch out two common profiles. Each of these athletes makes a fundamental error in failing to differentiate between gears while training and therefore falls short of optimal performance while racing.

Runner Profile #1: Speed Demon

Meet Speed Demon. Speed Demon lives by the motto, "Go hard or go home." For Speed Demon, training often becomes a race, even on recovery days when the aim is to go easy. Easy is truly a struggle for Speed Demon who detests doing "long slow distance." Speed Demon has started training with a heart rate monitor and personalized heart rate zones; but finds it difficult to stay in Zones 1-2 during lower intensity aerobic workouts—and often moves into higher zones for much of the time.[2]

Runner Profile #2: Endurance Monster

Meet Endurance Monster. Endurance Monster is the polar opposite of Speed Demon. Endurance Monster can plug along all day long in Zones 1-2, but has trouble unleashing a quick burst of speed to dash across a busy street even if their life depends upon it. Endurance Monster gets uncomfortable raising the heart rate above Zone 2 and views the higher zones as unknown and undesirable territory. A "fast sprint" for Endurance Monster is an oxymoron.

Despite their obvious differences, Speed Demon and Endurance Monster have a lot in common. They are both one-speed runners. They have the one gear they like and spend nearly all their training time in that gear. Yet they each seem to plateau in their training and fail to achieve the times they would like on race day. They each possess different elements needed for an effective training program, but neither has a complete program.

A complete and structured approach to training allows you to gain the numerous physiological adaptations needed for successful performance, which include increasing mitochondria (cellular factories for aerobic energy production) and capillary density in skeletal muscle, increasing stroke volume (the amount of blood pumped with each heart beat), improving aerobic capacity, effectively recruiting different muscle fiber types, improving coordination and efficiency of movement, developing the supporting structures (e.g. muscles, ligaments, tendons) needed to go fast, and building sport specific strength. A structured training program allows you to ramp up your fitness level from the beginning of base training to your most important race or races, ensuring that you do the work needed in the different training phases to optimize your race ready fitness.

Speed Demon would benefit from learning how to slow down on recovery days and put in the low intensity work foundational to aerobic training so that higher intensity days can truly hit the target goals and help ratchet up race ready fitness. Endurance Monster would benefit from learning how to speed up to put in the faster bursts of "true speed" needed to condition the intermediate and fast-twitch muscle fibers and to put in the bouts of higher intensity work needed to improve the ability to race faster with discomfort. As a result, both would enter onto a path toward faster performances.

HOW TO BUILD A COMPLETE RUNNING BASE

In outlining the ABCs of systematic training in *The Endurance Athlete's Guide*, I discuss the importance of establishing a strong aerobic foundation before moving into higher intensity anaerobic training that taps into the lactic acid system. This is the A in the ABC mnemonic, which stands for *aerobic before anaerobic.*

With this in mind, an emphasis during base training is placed on endurance runs in Zone 2.[3] These aerobic workouts are important for conditioning the body to better metabolize fat and spare glycogen (stored carbohydrate) as a long duration energy source.

Although these aerobic runs—often termed "long slow distance" (LSD)—are a vital component to base training, they are only part of the base building process. Of equal importance is the need to develop economy of movement while strengthening the muscles, ligaments and tendons that support your goal to run fast and efficiently. This is where the second part of the ABCs comes into play: B for *build endurance along with neuromuscular speed*.

By *neuromuscular speed*, I mean the firing of fast-twitch muscle fibers and coordination of proper movement patterns required for economy of motion. Note that this is different than the conception of "speed" as it is sometimes used to refer to activities of a few minutes in duration where the lactic acid system is tapped.

To build a complete running base, at least once or twice per week during base training you should incorporate drills and acceleration striders into easy runs or endurance runs.

Easy Runs

Easy runs are short runs (usually less than 30 minutes) in Zone 1. They are designed to aid recovery, add to your training volume and to loosen you up for the key runs of the week. Don't worry about pace or distance covered; the goal is to feel fresh at the end. Easy runs can incorporate a few minutes of drills and/or a few acceleration striders.

Endurance Runs

Endurance runs are aerobic runs in Zone 2 (i.e. conversational pace) of 20 minutes or longer. (The "long run" represents a longer version of this type of workout.) They are designed to provide the aerobic conditioning that is foundational to your fitness. You can incorporate the drills and striders detailed below into any endurance run of an hour or less in duration.

Running Drills

After you are warmed up, run through the following drills. Perform each drill 1-3 times for 20-40 meters. During the first few weeks, focus on the following four drills:

- Loosening Skips

- Side Skips

- Straight Leg Run

- Butt Kicks

Once you have mastered these first four drills; then add the next three drills to your repertoire:

- A Skip

- B Skip

- High Knees

Finally, when you are ready for more; add:

- Carioca (i.e. Grapevine)

- Carioca with High Knee

- Ankling

The full drill routine need only take about 10 minutes as part of your run. Keep your Garmin/watch running during the drill session and count the distance/time accumulated as part of your overall run time. This will incentivize you to think of this as a crucial component of these base training workouts (which it is!) rather than something extra or separate.

Acceleration Striders

At some point during the run (such as after drills), find a good 100 meter straightaway where you can do some acceleration striders. Ideally, this will be a softer surface, such as a track, the infield of a track, a grassy area such as a park, or an even section of dirt trail. Do 4-12 x 100 meter acceleration striders with the wind at your back—start off easy and gradually pick up your pace until you're at full speed by the end.

Focus on good form and leg turnover. These are "feel good sprints" to develop the neuromuscular action needed for good form and faster running. Gradually build your speed without straining for it. These will raise your heart rate, but will not keep it raised long enough to significantly tap into the lactic acid system. Jog 200-300 meters between each strider or until you feel fully recovered (with heart rate returned to zone 1) and ready for the next one. Don't worry about time or heart rate on these. These will help condition the fast-twitch and intermediate fast-twitch muscle fibers that even endurance athletes utilize during prolonged activity.

Notes on Implementation

Drills and acceleration striders provide important complementary elements to the low intensity aerobic work that comprises the bulk of your training volume. Note that the drills and striders do not necessarily need to occur together in the same runs. There are a variety of ways you can implement these elements into your base training. Aim to include drills into at least two runs per week; and aim to include striders into at least two runs per week. If you do this consistently during your base period, you will build a complete base that will effectively prepare you for faster training and racing down the road.

THE DYNAMIC WARMUP

Except for the rare athlete who has never suffered an injury, most runners are all too familiar with the pain associated with injuries to skeletal muscles. In fact, over 30 percent of the injuries treated in sports medicine clinics are muscular injuries. Yet warding off such injuries can be as simple as including a proper warmup into your training routine.

As widely recognized among coaches, athletes, and organizations such as the American College of Sports Medicine, a proper warmup affords the athlete many benefits prior to bouts of intense exercise. These benefits are summarized in a 2007 review article in the journal *Sports Medicine*,[4] which underscores the importance of the warmup in injury prevention.

Through raising the temperature of working muscles and increasing the diameter of blood vessels (vasodilation), the warmup increases blood flow through the body.

More oxygen is sent to working muscles in the service of energy production. The speed and force of muscle contractions increases, as does the speed of nerve transmissions. Flexibility is enhanced, and a protective mechanism is put in place whereby muscles require a greater force and length of stretch to produce a tear or strain.

Think of the classic analogy of a rubber band. A warm rubber band stretches further and faster than a cold one (which is more liable to snap apart).

So given the importance of warming up for injury prevention, what does a proper warmup look like?

Your warmup should take place within the 15 minutes that precede the main activity, and it should be tailored to the needs of that activity and the athlete.

For runners, the full dynamic run warmup includes three parts: (1) neuromuscular activation, (2) dynamic stretching, and (3) the cardiovascular component (i.e. light running).

Starting with some simple muscular recruitment exercises will help to "wake up" the communication lines between the nervous system and the muscular system to ready the body for activity.

Each exercise should be done at no more

than 20 percent effort—just enough to facilitate activation of the muscle group. Hold each exercise for 6 to 10 seconds; and do each one 2 to 3 times. The entire muscle activation sequence need only take 3 to 5 minutes at the very beginning of your workout. These can include some of the following.

Core Snap and Backward Lean

Start off by engaging the deep abdominals in your core. Imagine that your belly button is the front part of a metal snap that you might find on a jacket, and the back of that snap is located on your spine. Envision snapping that button closed.

To further facilitate deep abdominal activation, lean back on one leg and hold it for 6 to 10 seconds. Then switch to the other leg. Complete 2 to 3 repetitions on each leg.

Quadriceps Activation

To activate the quadriceps, balance on one leg while straightening the opposite one. Remember, the effort should be just enough to activate the muscle. Hold for 6 to 10 seconds; and switch to the other leg. Complete 2 to 3 repetitions on each leg.

Medial Glutes Activation

To activate the gluteus medius (medial hip muscles), balance on one leg while extending the other leg diagonally and to the side. Hold for 6 to 10 seconds; and switch to the other leg. Complete 2 to 3 repetitions on each leg.

Hip Flexors, Hamstrings, Glutes Activation

The last activation exercise consists of standing on one leg while bringing the opposite leg up so that the thigh is parallel to the ground. Hold this position for 6 to 10 seconds. Then, drive that leg back so that it is behind your body with the calf now parallel to the ground. Hold this for 6 to 10 seconds; then switch to the other leg. Complete 2 to 3 repetitions for each leg.

Progression toward Balance Drills

Once you have mastered these basic muscle activation exercises, you can gradually add an additional component to work on balance. Simply do each of the exercises just demonstrated using a balance disk. This will further enhance recruitment of core muscles.

Once you've completed the neuromuscular part of the warm up, you are ready to proceed into the dynamic stretching exercises.

Many readers will remember a time when "warming up" involved static stretching (i.e. relaxing a muscle, elongating it and holding it for a period of time). In fact, it is still not uncommon to see runners performing static stretches at the start of races or workouts.

Yet recent research has shown that static stretching prior to exercise can actually be detrimental to performance by weakening muscular strength. In their exercise guidelines, the American College of Sports Medicine advises against static stretching before workouts and competitions. To be sure, there is much debate around this issue; but general consensus has trended away from static stretching in favor of dynamic stretching as the best way to prepare the body for physical activity. Save the static stretching for after the workout. Use dynamic stretching before.

Dynamic stretching involves controlled movements that take joints through the ranges of motion that will be experienced during the coming workout. Rather than being passive (like static stretching), these movements are actively controlled by contracting muscles without forcing joints to move beyond the range they can comfortably achieve. Through multiple repetitions of the movement patterns, the muscles warm up and the range of motion is enhanced.

Below is a sequence of dynamic exercises that runners can use to warm up the muscles and enhance range of motion. Perform each exercise for 10 to 20 meters, moving from one to the next. If you feel particularly stiff or sore, then repeat as necessary. This second phase of the warm up need only take 3 to 10 minutes. These exercises can also be repeated at the end of the workout as part of the cooldown.

High Knee (Hurdle) Walk

Begin by walking with high knees for 10 to 20 meters.

Moving from the high knee walk, now add the hurdle component. Imagine you are stepping over the side of a hurdle as your walk. Drive with your knee and rotate around the hip joint. Do this for 10 to 20 meters.

Straight Leg Walk

For the straight leg walk, keep the leg straight and lift it up as high as you can by contracting the quads and hip flexors. As you bring your foot back to the ground, aim to finish with a slight scuffing or pawing motion. Never go to the point of strain nor force the movement. Only lift the leg as high as you can with comfort.

Backward Walk with Waist Bend

Starting in a standing position, hinge forward at the waist by pushing the butt backward. Return to the standing position, and take a half step backward with one foot. Hinge forward again at the waist. Return to the standing position, and take a half step backward with the other foot. Repeat this motion for about 10 meters to warm up your lower back and hamstrings.

Toe Walk and Heel Walk

For the toe walk, walk 10 to 20 meters on your toes. This will engage the calf muscles.

For the heel walk, walk 10 to 20 on your heels. This will engage the muscles on the front part of your lower leg (i.e. tibialis anterior).

Loosening Skips

Skip lightly while keeping your arms relaxed. Do this for 10 to 20 meters. Next, add forward arm circles for 10 to 20 meters. Switch to backward arm circles for 10 to 20 meters. Switch to forward arm circles with both arms for 10 to 20 meters. Switch to backward arm circles with both arms for 10 to 20 meters. Finally, open up the chest with a cross-chest arm swing for 10 to 20 meters.

Once you've completed the first two parts of the warmup—muscle activation and dynamic stretching—you are ready to proceed into the final cardiovascular phase. Run for 10 to 20 minutes at an easy pace with a few optional striders thrown in towards the end. The activity should elevate the heart rate and produce a light sweat.

If you are short on time, remember that the first two phases of the full warmup need only take 5 to 10 minutes before you delve into the actual running part of the warmup. Especially if you have experienced injuries in the past or if you run upon getting out of bed in the morning or after sitting at a desk all day, investing those extra minutes to prepare the body is time well spent. Remember, a proper warmup provides an important avenue for warding off injury.

THE PRE-RACE WARMUP

You've put in the training and now you're ready to toe the starting line for that running event. But one last question remains in your mind: how long should my warmup be? As the question assumes, some sort of warmup will be important to getting the most out of your race.

The warmup plays an important role in injury prevention and readies the body for the rigors of a race level intensity. Cold muscles are tight muscles; and tight muscles are more susceptible to strains and tears.

A warmup raises the temperature of working muscles. It leads to vasodilation, or the widening of blood vessels, which increases blood flow throughout the body. This sends more oxygen to working muscles to produce energy to fuel your activity. The speed of nerve transmissions increases, along with the speed and force of muscle contractions. And joint mobility and flexibility are enhanced.

In short, a proper warmup prepares the body to handle race level intensity from the time the starting gun fires.

As a general rule of thumb, the length of your warmup is inversely proportional to the length of the race. The shorter the race, the longer the warmup should be.

In shorter races (or even in intermediate distance races for elite runners), the intensity from the start will be high. To be able to match that intensity from the gun, the engine needs to be fully revved up so it can fire on all cylinders. This requires a warmup that starts early and includes some higher intensity running to raise the heart rate and get the muscles firing at race pace and faster.

In contrast, the longer the race, the shorter the warmup needs to be. In longer races (or even in shorter races for novice runners), the racing distance tends to exceed a day's typical training mileage. As a result, the intensity from the start is not as great. At these distances, the runner can use the beginning part of the race as an extension of the shorter warmup begun prior the starting gun. This especially applies to marathon racers who need a pre-race routine that provides a light warmup while conserving energy and muscle glycogen for the long effort ahead.

Regardless of the distance to be raced, I like to be at the race site at least an hour before the start. Even if you don't need a full hour to warm up, this will ensure you have time to take care of pre-race logistics such as checking in and taking care of your bib number, timing chip, toilet stops, etc. It really is amazing how fast time flies in the hour before a race. This is where a rehearsed routine will help you make the most of that time.

At the end of this chapter are some sample pre-race warmup protocols. Choose one that works best for the distance you will be racing, your experience level at that distance, and the amount of time you are afforded prior to the race.

If you show up late to the start, don't fret. In such cases, make the most of your time with the bare bones warmup and use the first part of the race as an extension of that warmup. This means you may need to adjust your race strategy a bit. Instead of going out at race pace, ease into that pace gradually after the first mile or so. You may even surprise yourself with a faster than expected performance due to the restraint you show in those early miles of the race.

The bottom line is that a good pre-race warmup gets your blood pumping and produces a light sweat. Find a routine that works for you and ritualize it before your races. This will lower pre-race anxiety and ensure you step on the starting line prepared for a good effort. Good luck, and remember to have fun!

Full Pre-Race Warmup for Shorter Races (e.g. 10K, 5K, 3200m, 1600m, 800m)

60 minutes prior	3-5 minutes of muscle activation exercises
55 minutes prior	3-5 minutes of dynamic stretching, leg swings
50 minutes prior	10-15 minutes of easy running at warmup pace
35 minutes prior	5 minutes of loosening skips and skipping drills
30 minutes prior	Use toilet (if needed), take off warmups, put on racing singlet/shoes
20 minutes prior	4 x 100m strides with 90 seconds jog between
10 minutes prior	Easy jog to starting area
5 minutes prior	Calm walk to starting line, shake out legs to stay loose on the line

Basic Pre-Race Warmup Shorter Races (e.g. 15K, 10K, 5K)

30 minutes prior	10-15 minutes of easy running at warmup pace
15 minutes prior	5 minutes of loosening skips, dynamic stretching, leg swings
10 minutes prior	2-3 x 100m strides with 90 seconds jog between
5 minutes prior	Calm walk to starting line

Full Pre-Race Warmup for Longer Races (e.g. Half Marathon, 15K, 10K)

60 minutes prior	5-10 minutes of easy walking
50 minutes prior	3-5 minutes of muscle activation exercises
45 minutes prior	3-5 minutes of dynamic stretching, leg swings
40 minutes prior	5-10 minutes of easy running at warmup pace
30 minutes prior	Use toilet (if needed), take off warmups, put on racing singlet/shoes
20 minutes prior	5-10 minutes of loosening skips and skipping drills
10 minutes prior	Easy jog to starting area
5 minutes prior	Calm walk to starting line

Basic Pre-Race Warmup Longer Races (Marathon, Half Marathon)

30 minutes prior	5-10 minutes of walking
20 minutes prior	5-10 minutes of easy running at warmup pace
10 minutes prior	5 minutes of loosening skips, dynamic stretching, leg swings
5 minutes prior	Calm walk to starting line

Bare Bones Pre-Race Warmup
for Late Arrivals

15 minutes prior	5-10 minutes of easy running at warmup pace
5 minutes prior	Calm walk to starting line

ESSENTIAL DRILLS TO IMPROVE YOUR RUNNING

Although it is easy to disregard technique as a valuable part of run training, dedicated attention to form holds substantial benefits, including greater resistance to injury and better running economy.

Runners who regularly incorporate drills into their training are better able to recruit muscles needed for the task, leaving them less injury prone. And when the going gets tough, they are more efficient. Given that an improvement to running economy is just as good as an improvement in VO_2max when it comes to that final number on the stopwatch, it only makes sense to squeeze as much "free speed" out of one's performance as possible.

The key to developing good form is to

ingrain proper movement patterns into your muscle memory so that they become automatic. And proper movements can be trained through drills. With proper movement patterns instilled as the default setting, you will be better prepared when fatigue threatens to break down your form.

Below is a sequence of running drills that you can easily incorporate into your run training. The drills are best performed on a soft surface, such as a rubberized track, the infield of a track, a flat dirt trail or grassy field.

Perform the drills after you have completed your initial warm up, or at the middle or end of your run. Do each drill for 10 to 20 meters, and go through the sequence at least once. If time permits, you can repeat the sequence 2 to 3 times. Aim to incorporate at least one to two drill sessions into your running program each week.

Running takes place almost exclusively in the sagittal plane (flexion/extension) to propel the runner forward, yet muscles that operate in the frontal plane (abduction/adduction) play an important role as stabilizers. These first two drills build strength and coordination among these stabilizing muscles.

Side-to-Side Skip

For the side-to-side skip, skip side to side by bringing your feet together and then shoulder width apart. Let your arms cross over each other in front of the body as you skip. Be sure to keep your hips and shoulders square—that is, they are perpendicular to the direction of motion.

Carioca, or Grapevine

Like the side-to-side skips, the carioca or grapevine drill further works the stabilizing muscles that play a secondary but nevertheless vital role in running. As you move sideways, cross one leg over the other in front and then behind. Hold your arms out to the side to begin; as you start to get the hang of the drill, use your arms as you would while running.

When you feel more comfortable, add a high knee component so that your front leg lifts up high as it moves across.

A Skip

These next drills recruit the primary movers—namely, the glutes and hamstrings—that operate during the active propulsion phase of the run. For the A skip, skip with high knees. As you bring your leg down, finish with a slight pawing motion as you pull backwards. This pawing motion is often neglected, but is a key element of a powerful stride. Focus on initiating that pull from the glutes as the hamstrings then join in the motion. This will ingrain the backward pulling motion important for running propulsion into your muscle memory. Use the same arm motion during this drill as you use while running.

B Skip

The B skip is nearly identical to the A skip, but first extends the leg forward. This extension of the leg dynamically stretches the hamstring and then allows you to really emphasize the backward pawing motion as your foot lands on the ground and pulls through. Get into the rhythm of the A and B skips by listening to the pattern of sound your feet make as they contact and scuff the ground, pawing backwards. Use the same arm motion during this drill as you use while running.

Butt Kicks

The butt kick drill further conditions and coordinates the glutes and hamstrings for a strong running stride. The butt kick drill should almost feel like a variation of running with high knees (rather than simply kicking backwards). Pull your heels up directly beneath you, keeping the knee, heel and toe up throughout the drill. Use the same arm motion during this drill as you use while running.

High Knees

The high knee drill works the loading phase

of the run. The key to performing the drill correctly is to focus on driving the foot down and letting it spring back up off the ground (rather than lifting the knees). Use the same arm motion during this drill as you use while running.

Straight Leg Run

The straight leg run is like the straight leg walk used during your dynamic warm up, only this time you are running. The straight leg run reinforces the important pawing motion practiced in the A skip and B skip. Start slowly and gradually increase your speed.

Avoid the temptation to lean backwards—in other words, keep your upper body perpendicular to the ground as you run with straight legs. As your foot contacts the ground, finish with that same backwards pawing motion as you practiced in the other drills—squeeze the glutes and hamstrings as you pull back on the track.

Ankling

The ankling drill helps facilitate the proper loading and spring during running. Starting at the toe, push the foot down so that the heel barely contacts the ground. The movement can be difficult to learn at first, so begin in slow motion; then gradually pick up the pace and keep the cadence high.

The bottom line is that good form equals free speed. Time-crunched athletes can easily work these drills into a few easy running days each week. As you do, focus on consistent practice and proper application to gain the most benefit for your running. The dividends will come in the form of better neuromuscular coordination and stronger muscles dedicated to the activity of running.

BUILDING STRONGER AND "SMARTER" MUSCLES

When most people think of strength training, they think of making their muscles stronger. But strong muscles aren't worth much if they don't fire when needed or coordinate with each other during sport specific movements. For endurance athletes engaged in strength training, it is important to recognize that stronger muscles form only part of the equation for enhanced performance. You also need to have good neuromuscular control over those muscles.

Any time a muscle contracts, it requires a signal from the nervous system. This is why we talk about neuromuscular movement (as opposed to just muscular movement). A great deal of the work done by the nervous system occurs more or less automatically as a result of patterns set down over time. We call this "muscle memory."

If you play the guitar, your fingers seem to "know" where to go to play a C chord, for example, without consciously placing them on the strings. Of course, it takes a while to build up mastery of those movement patterns. In general, it takes about 4,000-6,000 repetitions to change or develop new muscle memory patterns.

As athletes, the movements we make are built up over time in the same way. Poor form—and resulting injuries—can be a result of weak muscles, inhibition of muscles needed for a movement, or a combination of weak muscles that don't fire when needed. Functional strength work targets typical areas of muscular imbalances while teaching you to use those muscles in ways that carry over into your sport specific activities.

So to say we want to make our muscles "smart" as well as strong means that we're aiming to develop neuromuscular control in addition to strength. This is why it is always essential to perform the exercises—as well as your running—with proper form. You want to ingrain positive habits into your muscle memory.

Endurance athletes are eager to find ways to improve their performance, and many embrace strength training. Yet some of those who embrace strength training view it from a one sided perspective. For them, it is all about making muscles stronger without regard to function. If strength training doesn't involve heavy weights that target isolated muscle groups (e.g. machine weights); then they don't feel like they're getting a "good workout." Likewise, they see suggestions to incorporate supplemental functional work into daily activities in short spurts of a few minutes as too little or inconsequential to constitute a "good workout." For them, it is easy to blow off that daily ten minute functional strength session.

But if you shift your perspective on functional strength training to take in the broader picture of what we're trying to accomplish—stronger and smarter muscles— then it is easier to see the benefit of the supplemental work.

Let's return to the analogy of learning to play the guitar.

Imagine this scenario. Let's say you show up for your two hour guitar lesson once a week without picking up the guitar in between those weekly sessions. It takes the first part of the lesson to remember what you've forgotten over the past week. And by the end of the session, brain fatigue sets in and limits your ability to effectively practice the assigned chords. But you definitely walk away from the session feeling like you got the equivalent of a "good workout." Your fingers hurt, you're tired, etc.

Now image this scenario. You still dedicate two hours a week to practicing your guitar, but now your weekly lesson takes one hour and you spend ten minutes each day in between the weekly lessons practicing the movement patterns for the chords assigned that week. In each of those ten minute daily sessions, you may not feel like you're getting the equivalent of a "good workout," but you gradually begin to learn the chords. And you do so sooner than in the first scenario.

Contrasting these two scenarios underscores the point that making your muscles smarter benefits from consistent, frequent reinforcement of the neuromuscular patterns that contribute to muscle memory. If it takes 4,000-6,000 repetitions to ingrain movement patterns into muscle memory, it is best to spread those repetitions out in short but frequent sessions rather than lumping them all together in longer but infrequent sessions.

The bottom line? Don't think it is inconsequential to incorporate short but frequent functional strength sessions or neuromuscular drills into your daily activities. I am a big advocate of investing a few extra minutes a day into "bonus" or "secret" training. Step away from the desk during the workday to do a few minutes of planks or donkey kicks or balance drills, for example.

It may seem like nothing when you are training up to eight, twelve, fifteen or more hours a week in endurance activities. But attention to this supplemental work will help you reinforce movement patterns needed for good neuromuscular control.

When it comes to optimal performance come race day, your muscles need to be more than strong. They also need to be smart!

FUNCTIONAL STRENGTH WORK IN 10 MINUTES A DAY

The principle of specificity states that runners must dedicate substantial training time to running. Yet spending all your training time in this pursuit is a recipe for overuse injuries. This is where supplemental strength training becomes an indispensable tool in the runner's repertoire. Functional strength work can help runners of all levels overcome muscular imbalances en route to becoming stronger, more efficient, and less injury prone.

And the best news is that even a little supplemental work can go a long way. Time-crunched runners need only dedicate an extra 10 minutes several days per week to make a difference. If you can't spare any extra time before or after your running sessions, then consider squeezing in that 10 minutes before breakfast in the morning (a great way to start the day and get the blood flowing), while taking a break from work in the afternoon (a great way to alleviate the stress of sitting at a desk), or while watching your favorite television show in the evening (use the commercials as training intervals).

Below are several exercises to implement into your training routine.

Body Squats

Start with feet shoulder width apart.

Put your shoulder blades "in your back pockets" so you are standing tall.

Keeping your back flat, push your hips backwards as you bend slightly at the knees. Here, you are "hinging" from the hips as you go into a squat. Keep your weight over your heels.

As you squat (again, keeping the back flat and hinging from the hips), raise your arms out in front as a counter balance.

Go to parallel or deeper as long as you can maintain the flat back.

Squeeze the glutes and return to a standing position.

The key is to initiate the movement by hinging at the hips with a flat back. You should feel your glutes working (not the quads). Done properly, this is a glute exercise!

Perform 1-5 sets of 8-12 reps. Or, perform 1-5 sets of 20-40 second intervals (doing as many reps as possible during those intervals).

Single Leg Squats

Running is effectively a series of alternating single leg squats. Improve your coordination and strength with these single leg squats and you will become a better runner!

Doing this in front of a mirror is helpful to monitor form.

Start with a firm foundation on one leg (weight evenly distributed over forefoot and rear foot). Lift other leg up.

Pushing the hips backward (hinging from the hips), bend slight at the knee to go into a squat.

Go as far as you can without breaking form. Proper form means you move straight down and up (as in a double leg squat) without letting your knee or hips dive in or out and without losing balance or foot contact.

Think quality! Only perform as many single leg squats as you can with perfect form. Start with one and progress from there. Balance drills and hip/glute strengthening with other exercises will help improve your ability to do single leg squats.

Good Mornings

Start with feet shoulder width apart.

Put your shoulder blades "in your back pockets" so you are standing tall.

Keeping your back flat with knees slightly bent, push your hips backwards to "hinge" from the hips. Keep your weight over your heels and eyes looking forward (not downward). Bend as far as your range of motion allows with a straight back (stop if your back starts to round).

Squeeze the glutes and return to a standing position.

You want to primarily feel the glutes working (rather than the lower back). If you are feeling your lower back working, focus on squeezing the glutes to shift the workload to the butt.

Perform 1-5 sets of 8-12 reps per leg. Or, perform 1-5 sets of 20-40 second intervals (doing as many reps as possible during those intervals).

Front Plank

Lie in prone position (face down).

Place toes on ground in dorsiflexed position.

Place elbows under shoulders.

Squeeze the quads. Squeeze the glutes. And

rise into a plank.

Keep back flat. Do not let butt rise or sink. Stay flat.

Hold for 30 seconds to 3 minutes, breaking up with rest as needed.

Front Plank with Straight Leg Hip Extension

This combines the front plank with straight leg hip extensions. In other words, you perform straight leg hip extensions from the front plank position.

To get into the front plank position: Lie in prone position (face down). Place toes on ground in dorsiflexed position. Place elbows under shoulders. Squeeze the quads. Squeeze the glutes. And rise into a plank. Keep back flat. Do not let butt rise or sink. Stay flat.

Now, squeeze one glute to vertically raise that leg. Keep the back flat and still. Initiate and complete the movement from the glute.

If you feel the lower back or hamstring working, work on straight leg hip extensions while lying on the ground before progressing to the plank position. This should work the glute.

Perform 1-5 sets of 8-12 reps per leg. Or, perform 1-5 sets of 20-40 second intervals (doing as many reps as possible during those intervals).

Lying Hip Abductions

(a.k.a. Side/Lying Leg Raises or Jane Fondas)

Lie on side. Stack top foot on top of bottom foot. Dorsiflex (bring toes to knee) and slightly pigeon toe top foot (this is the position to keep your foot in for the raises).

Squeeze medial glute (side of hip) to raise leg as high as you can. Lower leg back down in a controlled manner. Repeat.

Perform 1-5 sets of 8-12 reps per leg. Or, perform 1-5 sets of 20-40 second intervals (doing as many reps as possible during those intervals).

Standing Hip Abductions

These are a standing version of the Lying Hip Abductions (aka Side/Lying Leg Raises or "Jane Fondas").

The standing version engages more core muscles as you balance on one leg.

Stand on one foot. Maintain tall and straight body position.

Squeeze medial glute (side of hip) to abduct (move away from body) as far as you can. Return leg to midline in a controlled manner. Repeat.

Perform 1-5 sets of 8-12 reps per leg. Or,

perform 1-5 sets of 20-40 second intervals (doing as many reps as possible during those intervals).

Side Plank

Lie on side.

Put top foot in front of bottom foot (easier) or stack top foot on top of bottom foot (harder).

Push up into a side plank (use top hand if needed as a brace).

Use hand as a brace (easiest). Move hand to hips (harder). Raise hand in air (hardest).

Hold for 30 seconds to 3 minutes per side, breaking up with rest as needed.

Side Plank with Hip Abduction

This combines the side plank with lying hip abductions. In other words, you perform hip abductions (side leg raises) from the side plank position.

To get into the side plank position: Lie on side. Stack top foot on top of bottom foot. Push up into a side plank.

Now, squeeze the medial glute (side of hip) to raise leg as high as you can. Lower leg back down in a controlled manner. Repeat.

Perform 1-5 sets of 8-12 reps per leg. Or,

perform 1-5 sets of 20-40 second intervals (doing as many reps as possible during those intervals).

Superman

Start in the prone position (lying face down).

Lift your left arm and right leg off the ground.

As you place your left arm and right leg back on the ground, raise your right arm and left leg off the ground.

Alternate this motion for time (e.g. 20-30 seconds) or for a designated number of reps (e.g. 10-20).

Back Extension

Start lying on the floor in the prone position (face down).

Pull your elbows into the rib cage and lift upper body off the ground, leading with the chest.

Squeeze the shoulder blades.

Return upper body to the ground.

Repeat for a designated time (e.g. 20-30 seconds) or number of reps (e.g. 8-12).

Eccentric Calf Raise

Rise up with both legs and down with one leg.

3 x 30 reps per leg per day

Week 1: body weight to flat

Week 2: body weight to drop (done on stair or slant board)

Week 3-6: progressively add weight in a backpack up to 45-55 pounds

These are done daily for 6 weeks to repair chronic Achilles tendinopathy.

RECONNECT WITH YOUR MOST IMPORTANT RUNNING MUSCLES

If you're wondering right off the bat what I consider your most important running muscles, here's the answer: your glutes.

The *gluteus maximus* (or glute max) initiates hip extension. And running is all about hip extension. Sure, the hamstrings are involved in extending the hips as well. But they cannot carry the burden alone. They require the more powerful glutes to get into the game.

Plus, the glutes, with their greater percentage of slow-twitch fibers, are well positioned to contribute to both hip extension and core stability while running. This translates into a more effective and powerful stride...and more speed.

Unfortunately, runners in this day and age have numerous strikes against them when it comes to engaging their glutes. Excessive amounts of sitting "turn off" the glutes and inhibit their firing when you get out of that chair. Too much sitting can also result in tight hip flexors, making full hip extension difficult to attain. Plus, traditional running shoes with elevated heels tend to shift runners toward a quad-dominant firing pattern with less reliance on the glutes.

Yet sidelining the glutes during running is exactly what you don't want. If your goal is to optimize your gait for performance and injury prevention, you need to put the mantra run from the glutes into practice. This means paying attention to supplemental drills and exercises that will allow you to strengthen your glutes and get them firing properly when running.

Here are some functional strength exercises that target those glutes.

Glute Bridge

Lie on back with knees bent.

Squeeze glutes (butt) and rise up into a bridge. Return to ground in controlled manner.

Note: the muscles working should be the glutes (butt), not the quads (front of leg) or lower back. Be sure to initiate the movement by squeezing the glutes.

Perform 1-5 sets of 8-12 reps per leg. Or, perform 1-5 sets of 20-40 second intervals (doing as many reps as possible during those intervals).

Single Leg Glute Bridge

Lie on back with knees bent.

Lift one leg up or place across opposite knee.

Squeeze glute and rise up into a bridge. Return to ground in controlled manner.

Note: the muscle working should be the glute (butt), not the quads (front of leg) or lower back. Be sure to initiate the movement by squeezing the glute.

Perform 1-5 sets of 8-12 reps per leg. Or, perform 1-5 sets of 20-40 second intervals (doing as many reps as possible during those intervals).

Donkey Kicks

Get on the floor on hands and knees. Keep back straight as with the plank.

Keeping back flat and still, squeeze the glute to move one leg back and slightly to the side (like a donkey kicking).

Note: the movement should be initiated from the glute (butt), not the lower back. If you feel the lower back working instead, start with smaller movements until you can increase the range of extension using only the glute.

Perform 1-5 sets of 8-12 reps per leg. Or, perform 1-5 sets of 20-40 second intervals (doing as many reps as possible during those intervals).

Throw Out Your Desk Chair

Throw out your desk chair? Well, completely ditching it may be a bit extreme. But it might be time to give it up at least on a part-time basis. Here's why. Chairs are making our lives miserable and sitting too much is literally killing us.

If sitting were considered a sport, we would be overtraining big time. Most would consider training for eight hours or more per day five days a week as overdoing it. Running for eight hours a day five days a week? Even ultrarunners have their limits. But many of us don't think twice about sitting for up to eight hours or more per day in front of a computer at a desk. Not to mention the hours we log sitting in a car, on a couch in front of a TV, etc.

And all this sitting is unhealthy. Research suggests that extended sitting is associated with increased risk of chronic health and metabolic problems, including cardiovascular disease and type 2 diabetes.[5]

And if you think you can counterbalance excessive sitting by going out and training for 30 minutes, an hour, two hours or even three or four hours, consider this. Even if you worked out for three hours a day versus sitting at your desk for six hours, sitting would beat working out by a two to one margin. And "epidemiologic evidence suggests that sitting time has deleterious cardiovascular and metabolic effects that are independent of whether adults meet physical activity guidelines."[6]

I know. Most runners don't readily qualify as "sedentary" individuals and may possess more immunity than most in our sedentary society to the worst of these health problems. Yet even setting aside the research cited here, sitting too much can negatively impact athletes in another way—namely, by giving athletic overuse injuries a head start through poor postural habits.

As the twig bends so grows the tree. The typical slouched position at a desk in front of a computer often involves protracted neck, internally rotated shoulders and little engagement from core muscles. And these habits of posture—along with accompanying muscle tightness and weakness—are often carried over into other daily activities, including our athletic endeavors.

Piriformis, glute, hamstring or IT band problems while running? Chances are your sitting has given you a case of "sleepy glutes." Key supporting muscles may be weak or fail to fire properly while running. Again, too much sitting can provide those athletic injuries with a nice head start.

So what can be done?

Functional strength exercises are one important step to take to counteract muscular imbalances caused by too much sitting. However, all those hours of sitting cannot simply be undone by a limited amount of strength training. It is also crucial that we incorporate positive postural habits into all our daily activities, including—of course—sitting.

When you are sitting, be sure to sit with good posture. Back straight. Shoulder blades pulled back and down. Head retracted with ears in line with the shoulders (rather than head protracted forward). And if you must sit for prolonged periods of time, be sure to get up and walk around frequently (every half hour or so). The point is to break up the long sitting sessions with some movement that gets the blood flowing and muscles working while reinforcing good posture.

When sitting at a desk, consider using a balance ball (cheaper than an office chair anyway) part of the time instead of a typical desk chair. A balance ball will force you to engage your core muscles (abdominals, back, hips, glutes) while you sit, allowing you to be more active and burn more calories. Be sure to sit with a straight back and good posture, a habit that should then be carried over to sitting in a normal chair when you do that.

If possible, consider using a stand up desk arrangement—at least part of the time—to break up long periods of sitting while at work. Stand on one leg at a time while keeping your hips level, shifting back and forth between each leg. Think of this as a "bonus" or "secret" training session of single leg balance drills.

And if you watch TV at night, perform some core functional strength or flexibility work during commercial breaks. Not only does this eliminate some sitting time, but it will also give you an opportunity to counteract those weak areas caused by excessive sitting. Try, for example, some side planks, side leg raises, side planks with leg raises, or single leg glute bridges. Even 10 minutes a day can be beneficial. Start with an introductory routine and gradually work towards an advanced routine. You can even throw in some of these exercises during breaks from sitting throughout the work day.

Whether or not you actually ditch the desk chair, becoming more aware of your sitting habits will allow you to find ways to mitigate the deleterious effects that excessive sitting can have on your health and athletic performance. Keep in mind that sitting, like most things in life, is best done in moderation.

Maximizing Body Position for Economical Running

A common piece of advice given to runners is to "run tall." To grasp what this looks like, imagine a straight line draw from your ankles through your ears. While running, you want to maintain a "tall" body position so that at full leg extension, a line runs more or less from the ankles up through the knees, hips, shoulders, and ears.

While running tall, a slight lean comes from the ankles. In other words, the ankles act as the pivot point (not the hips). This subtle lean allows the runner to take advantage of gravity to maintain forward momentum.

You can get a feel for running tall with a slight forward lean by working with a running partner. Here's how. Stand so you and your partner face each other. Partner A places their arms into the running position. Partner B holds their hands about an inch in front of Partner A's upper chest (below the shoulders), ready to take the weight of Partner A. Partner A then drops their torso forward—leaning from the ankles—and falls into Partner B's hands.

Again, the lean is slight and the ankles are the pivot point (do not hunch forward at the waist!). Hold this for several seconds to get a feel for this position. Make sure you are not allowing yourself to bend forward at the waist; let your partner hold your weight.

Once you and your partner have traded roles a few times, add the next component of the progression. With Partner A leaning into Partner B, Partner B steps to the side as Partner A carries momentum from the lean into a run for about 10 meters. Be sure to start with a short step to ensure the tall body position with the slight lean is maintained. The key is to carry this body position into the run.

The final component of the progression is the partner high knee drill. Start again with Partner A leaning into Partner B. Now, Partner A drives forward with high knees as Partner B provides resistance while walking/jogging backward. After about 10 meters, Partner B steps to the side, and Partner A carries the form into a run for another 20 meters. The key here is for Partner A to maintain the body position and momentum from the forward lean into the run.

Another variation on the partner high knee drill is to use a running harness. You can either have a partner provide resistance by holding the harness from behind or attach the harness to a tire (no partner required) that you drag behind you.

Remember that good form in your run training holds substantial benefits, including greater resistance to injury and better running economy. Investing some extra time dedicated to drills such as those described above will eventually pay off with the dividend of "free speed."

CORE CONTROL AND POSTURAL STABILITY FOR RUNNERS

The glute max, along with the hamstrings, act as primary hip extensors. And each step you take while running involves extension of the hips. In today's world dominated by sitting, it is easy for the glutes to become neglected and underused. As a result, it is not uncommon for runners to shift the burden of hip extension onto the hamstrings. This is bad news because runners who rely on their hamstrings at the expense of the glute max give up a great deal of efficiency—not to mention increase the potential for injury.

Although the hamstrings and glute max are both effective at extending the hips during running, the hamstrings are comprised of a greater percentage of fast-twitch muscle fibers whereas the glute max contains a greater percentage of slow-twitch muscle fibers. Slow-twitch fibers excel at long duration activities—like extending your hip step after step while running long distances. The glute max, like the Energizer Bunny, is better equipped for the long haul.

In addition, the glute max is a far more powerful muscle than the hamstring. With these characteristics, the glute max is crucial to maintaining the pelvis in a stable, neutral position while running—or while walking or simply standing for that matter.

Remember the key tenets of good running posture. Maintain a tall body with a slight forward lean from the ankles. Instability in the core can easily disrupt this posture, which is why effective runners must possess a strong core.

It is not uncommon to see runners with an excessive lumbar arch while running. This means the pelvis is tilted forward, which overlengthens the hamstrings. When the glute max clocks out or fails to report for duty, the hamstrings are not only left to carry the burden of hip extension, but they are asked to do this in an overlengthened state as a result of the anterior pelvic tilt. This can be a pain in the butt or hamstring—quite literally.

To eliminate excessive lumbar arch, focus on increasing the flexibility of the hip flexors along with work that strengthens and cues the deep abdominals (transversus abdominis) and glute max. Through the functional strength exercises and muscle activation cues recommended below, the aim is to feel more like you are "running from the butt" with the glute max initiating each step.

Since half of this neuromuscular work is about making the muscles smarter—that is, firing when needed—and not just stronger, it will also be helpful to cue the deep abdominals and glutes throughout the day while walking and standing during everyday activities (especially after long periods of sitting). This will help "retrain" the core muscles necessary for good posture and economical running.

Functional Strength Exercises

- Front planks to target deep abdominals

- Glute bridge, donkey kicks and other exercises that strengthen and cue the glute max

- Advance to leg raises from front plank position as an alternative to the above

Muscle Activation Cues

- Perform a minute or two of front plank before running to cue and engage deep abdominals

- Perform a few sets of donkey kicks before running to cue and engage glute max
- Neuromuscular activation exercises that cue the glute max

OVERCOMING DROPPED HIPS FOR BETTER RUNNING FORM

Are you a runner that has dealt with your share of iliotibial (IT) band or knee problems? Are you a new or veteran runner who would like to avoid those problems? Evidence suggests that many of these problems can be overcome by addressing a key weakness that numerous runners exhibit: weak hips.[7]

Running is an activity that takes place primarily in the sagittal plane—meaning that movement occurs forwards and backwards. We rely on flexors and extensors such as the hamstrings and quadriceps as primary movers to propel us through the sagittal plane toward the finish line. Yet a key element of good running form involves the muscles that operate in the frontal (coronal) plane—namely, the hip abductors (gluteus medius, gluteus minimus) and the hip external rotators. These muscles act as important stabilizers vital to supporting our forward movement.

Here's a simple test to check the strength of your hip abductors. Stand on one leg and note what happens to your hip opposite your planted leg. Does it have a tendency to drop? Or, do you lean your upper body to the side of your planted leg (which might raise your opposite hip)? If do you either of these, the hip stabilizers on the side of the planted leg are weak or not firing.

This is because when your right leg, for example, is raised with your left foot planted on the ground, your right hip is projected over to that side of the body without any support directly beneath it. Like a deck cantilevered over a river (think Frank Lloyd Wright's "Fallingwater"), support must come from the non-cantilevered side. In the case of your hips, the support comes from the stabilizing muscles in your stance leg—notably, the gluteus medius and gluteus minimus.

As we run forward through the sagittal plane, we are effectively alternating between single leg stances—left leg, right leg, left leg, right leg—mile after mile, day after day, week after week, year after year. Without strong hip abductors, the opposite hip drops and increases the forces on the IT band and knee of the stance leg. If you put in enough miles while running like this, overuse injuries will eventually result. This is why good running is more than just an aesthetic nicety. It is an important component of injury prevention—not to mention that good form leads to improved efficiency, which translates into faster times with less work ("free speed").

As any runner knows, towards the end of a race everything starts to fatigue. The trick is to build adequate strength and neural patterns so that once the fatigue starts to set in, the hip stabilizers can continue doing what they should be doing to maintain form.

Since it is quite common for many runners to have weaker hip abductors than adductors, it is important to address this strength imbalance through the addition of core exercises that target the gluteus medius and minimus, such as side leg raises (i.e. lying hip abductions).

In addition, running drills that target movement in the frontal (coronal) plane are important elements of a comprehensive running program. This includes side skips and (high knee) carioca drills.

Finally, even if one has strong hip abductors, they are no good if they do not fire when needed. When skeletal muscles are used, there is both a neural component and a muscular component. The nervous system has to first send signals to the skeletal muscle to initiate the contraction. You can "wake up" this communication line by performing some simple

neuromuscular activation before runs. ⌐
reinforce the pattern through the
mentioned above.

And if you want some bonus training, ditch
that chair and stand when you're at your desk—
one leg at a time, alternating sides. Or if you're
not quite ready to give up the chair, practice
single leg balance drills throughout the day
during regular activities, such as brushing your
teeth or standing in line at the store. Just be sure
to keep your hips level as you practice your
single leg stances (no dropping and no cheating
by leaning your trunk to the side of the planted
leg!).

OPTIMIZE YOUR STRIDE RATE FOR MORE EFFICIENT RUNNING

One thing that all elite distance runners have in common is a remarkably similar stride rate. They run at a cadence of about 90 or more steps per foot each minute. This cadence remains similar whether it's the start of a race, the middle or the finishing kick. The rest of us can learn from their example.

A quicker cadence has several advantages. Among them is spreading out the impact forces involved in running. To illustrate, imagine that you are trying to jump from one end of a room to the other. If you wanted to do so while dishing out the least amount of landing shock to your body, would you choose three big hops or ten smaller hops? As you guessed, the smaller, shorter hops would get you there with less jarring of the joints.

It's the same with running. The more steps a runner takes per minute, the less impact there is per foot strike. In addition, it is harder to overstride when running with a quicker cadence. So a quicker cadence helps eliminate that deleterious braking action associated with overstriding. Given that many running injuries are brought about by landing impact, one can see how a quicker cadence can be advantageous in terms of preventing injuries.

The first step towards optimizing your stride rate is to find out where you currently stand. On your next run, take several counts of your cadence throughout the workout. Choose one foot—left or right—and count how many times it contacts the ground in 20 or 30 seconds. Multiply your 20-second count by three or your 30-second count by two to get your per minute cadence.

If your cadence is less than 28-30 foot strikes per 20 seconds, 42-45 per 30 seconds, or 84-90 per minute; then try to shorten your stride and increase the cadence. Try to get as close as you can to 90 foot strikes per minute. Count your foot strikes periodically to check your progress. When you find a good rhythm within the target range, set the internal metronome in your head to that frequency and let your feet follow.

Quickening your cadence may feel a bit strange if you currently have a slow turnover. It may take some time to reset your internal metronome. As you work on it, it can be helpful to watch video of a runner like Haile Gebraselassie and visualize his turnover in your mind on your runs.

Pay particular attention to your cadence on easy runs or long, slow distance runs. These are where many people have a tendency to slow down the stride rate along with the running pace. But this is actually the ideal time to practice your quicker cadence! You can keep the pace easy with a high cadence—it just requires shorter steps.

Remember that regardless of your pace, the cadence should remain more or less the same. Whether you are running intervals or doing a recovery jog in between those intervals, keep the turnover consistent. This will ingrain the turnover rate into your muscle memory. Developing habits of good form in your training translates into better performance when you're really tired at the end of those races.

Tips for High Altitude Trail Running

There's nothing quite like running on mountain trails to experience the freedom of running and the breathtaking beauty of the world. And racing on high altitude trails adds a whole new dimension to the competitive challenge of running, dishing out steep ascents and elevation gains that are rarely found in tamer road races. If you are a road racer ready for a change of scenery, keep these tips in mind as you head up high to test your mettle against challenging new terrain.

Go out Conservatively

For races at altitude—and especially races with an uphill start at altitude—start out slower than usual. Less available oxygen for your lungs at higher altitude means you can run into oxygen debt that much quicker. And once you do, it can take longer to repay that debt.

Keep a High Cadence

As gravity takes its toll and slows your pace, keep the cadence high. Think short but quick steps to maintain a good rhythm and proper form to propel your body upwards and onward.

Make Gradual Moves while Climbing

As you focus on catching those competitors just up the trail, be patient and increase your pace gradually to reel them in. Fast uphill surges can often prove counterproductive.

Plan for Irregular Aid Stations

Typically, the more challenging the course, the more difficult it may be for race directors to provide frequent support. Even if aid stations are as frequent as you would expect for a road race of the same distance, the slower pace of high altitude trail running means it will take you longer to get from one to another.

Pre-hydrate and Stay Hydrated/Fueled

Higher altitudes bring dryer air and the susceptibility of fluid/electrolyte loss. Prehydrate in the days before the race and stay hydrated and fueled during the race. Depending upon the frequency of aid stations, consider carrying a small water bottle and a few gels so you can drink/fuel at regular intervals.

Be Prepared for Shifts in the Weather

Some races at higher altitudes require runners to carry a jacket. Even if they don't, and you anticipate being on the course for a while, it's a good idea to be well prepared for summer thunderstorms (or even snowstorms) that move into the mountains in the afternoon.

Make the Most of the Downhill Sections

Unless you're doing an ascent with a mountaintop finish, what goes up must come down. Use gravity to your advantage. Keep a high cadence, stay alert, and maintain good footing to make the most of the downhill sections.

Finally, breathe deeply and enjoy the beauty around you!

Rethink Traditional Running Shoe Assumptions

Part of the beauty of running is its simplicity. The only piece of equipment that most runners require is a good pair of running shoes. Strap shoes on your feet and you're good to go!

But what constitutes a good pair of running shoes? More importantly, what running shoes are best for you given your particular needs? In light of recent attention given to barefoot running and minimalist shoe designs, what exactly do shoes do for you anyway? And what should you look for as a runner interested in comfort, performance, and injury prevention?

My aim here is to provide you with a guide to running shoes based on the latest evidence found in peer-reviewed academic journals and utilized by up-to-date biomechanists, physical therapists, and running coaches. Along the way, I outline the traditional (outdated) view on running shoe design and prescription—a perspective that is still alive and well when you walk into many running shoe stores today—and argue for a new, simple set of guidelines that you can use to ensure the running shoes you purchase meet your needs as a runner. After all, why spend hundreds of dollars on running shoes unless they support your needs?

The Traditional View on Choosing Running Shoes

Let's start by taking a look at the traditional view on choosing running shoes, which starts with arch type. From a clinical perspective, this view is easy to implement because it provides three neat categories for classifying foot types: high arch, medium arch, low arch. Determining which category you fit into is as easy as having someone look at your arches while standing (or standing on pavement with wet feet and examining the footprint). These foot types are then associated with the amount of pronation assumed to occur upon foot strike.

Pronation refers to the inward movement of your foot upon landing. Pronation is what allows your body to absorb the shock of your footfall. Pronation is necessary for adequate shock absorption; but excess pronation—called *overpronation*—has been thought to lead to common running injuries (e.g. plantar fasciitis, shin splints, knee problems). The traditional view assumes that flatter feet overpronate and that this excess motion needs to be controlled through shoe features. This leads to the three types of shoes you find when you go into the running shoe store:

1. *Neutral, or cushioned shoes*. Neutral, or cushioned shoes have a uniform color and uniform density throughout the midsole, and are built on a curved last. These types of shoes are prescribed for neutral runners and underpronators (and also for the rare supinator) with normal to high arches.

2. *Stability shoes*. You can spot a stability shoe by picking it up and looking at the medial (inner) side. You will often see a darker color (gray) or some sort of plug, often called a medial post. This darker material is denser than the surrounding (white) material. The principle behind stability shoes is that the denser material is supposed to slow down the pronation (i.e. inward movement) of the foot when landing on the heel. Stability shoes are usually built on a semi-curved last to accommodate some arch.

3. *Motion control shoes.* Motion control shoes are more extreme than stability shoes. As with stability shoes, you'll find the darker (denser) material and/or plug on the medial side in an attempt to control pronation. In addition, the shoes are built on a straight last to accommodate low arches or flat feet. They are almost like buying shoes with built-in orthotics.

Another common design feature of traditional running shoes is an elevated heel. Typically, a two to one ratio is common with the heel being twice as high as the toe. The heel is where all that cushy material is placed for shock absorption in an effort to ostensibly attenuate impact forces.

Craig Richards and colleagues dub shoes with these traditional design elements "Pronation control, Elevated Cushioned Heel" (PECH) running shoes.[8] They conducted a comprehensive review of the scholarly literature for studies that would support the prescription of PECH shoes based on foot type. What they found should surprise many who advocate the traditional view: *there is no research evidence to support the prescription of PECH shoes for injury prevention.*

Their review does not mean these types of traditional running shoes are necessarily ineffective, but it does mean that there is no scientific evidence to support the traditional model of shoe prescription and design that has become common wisdom in the running shoe industry over the past three plus decades.

Challenging the Traditional Model of Running Shoe Prescription and Design

If we look more closely at the traditional assumptions of running shoe prescription and design, recent studies provide evidence that PECH shoes are not all that the marketing hype makes them out to be. J.J. Knapik and colleagues, for example, demonstrate that prescribing shoe types (cushioned, stability, motion-control) based on arch types (high, medium, low) has little influence on injury prevention.[9]

Part of the ineffectiveness could come from the assumption that the amount of pronation during running neatly correlates with foot type. Remember, the traditional view prescribes shoe type (cushioned, stability, motion-control) based on foot type (high, medium, low arch). The assumptions are that the foot type can act as a window into how much the foot pronates while running, and that this pronation needs to be controlled.

However, Jay Dicharry and colleagues show that tests done to assess foot structure while standing do not neatly predict what the foot does while running.[10] Again, there is little indication that someone with any one of the three standardized foot types would benefit from the industry's corresponding shoe types as tools for injury prevention.[11]

With regard to the elevated cushioned heel in traditional shoes, we do know from studies that such features negatively impact proprioception and joint stability.[12]

Proprioception refers to the ability to sense and feel the position, location, and orientation of the body (and its parts) during movement. When running, a foot's proprioception guides it into position upon landing to absorb impact forces and provide stability to the joint. In effect, all that cushy material in those elevated heels of traditional running shoes detracts from the ability of the foot to do its job.

Further, the assumption that increased cushioning material in shoes translates into lower impact forces upon landing has been shown to be incorrect.[13] To the contrary, the more cushioning in the shoe, the harder the foot tends to land. The mechanoreceptors in the foot—which are sense organs involved in proprioception—have difficulty working effectively when a thick layer of cushioning material lies between the foot and the ground.

In addition, elevating the heel shifts foot loading forward, which leads to a quad-dominant firing pattern with less reliance on the gluteus maximus. Shifting the workload to the quads while inhibiting the firing of the glutes results in anterior pelvic tilt and excessive arch in the lower back.[14] As I've discussed in a previous article that examines the role of the glutes in running, when the pelvis tilts forward and there is excessive lower back arch, an overlengthening of the hamstrings results. When the glute max clocks out or fails to report for duty, the hamstrings are not only left to carry the burden of hip extension, but they are asked to do this in an overlengthened state as a result of the anterior pelvic tilt. This can be a pain in the butt or hamstring—quite literally.

Improper muscle firing patterns are an important culprit behind many running overuse injuries. Yet traditional running shoes only contribute to the problem of inactive glutes (a problem also compounded by excessive amounts of sitting) and detract from functional stability. Much of the functional strength training, neuromuscular activation exercises, and drills for runners are aimed at ingraining healthy movement patterns into muscle memory, including (re)training the glutes to fire as needed for an effective (injury free) running stride. Wouldn't it be nice if your shoes didn't work against this effort?

In sum, scientific studies to support the traditional PECH running shoe model are conspicuously absent. At the same time, numerous studies show the negative repercussions of elevated heels and excessive cushioning while also emphasizing the ineffectiveness of PECH shoes in preventing common running injuries.

The Foot Strike Debate

At this point, it is perhaps necessary to address the issue of fore-foot/mid-foot versus rear-foot landing. It is necessary because this issue has generated intense debate in the running community. Unfortunately, in my view, the debate (although interesting) acts as a bit of a red herring. It can detract from more central issues in choosing running shoes.

Given the current state of research, I believe it is best to take an agnostic position when it comes to foot strike. There simply isn't enough evidence to conclusively argue for one pattern over another. Substantial variability exists among both shod and barefoot runners, and there are pros and cons to the different patterns. It is difficult to argue for a one-size-fits-all solution in this area. Whether one first lands on the heel or contacts with the mid-foot or fore-foot before lowering the heel depends upon many variables unique to the individual runner's needs, situation, and even skill. With that said, let's look at what we do know with regard to foot strike patterns during running.

The place to start is the research conducted by Daniel Lieberman and colleagues,[15] made famous by the barefoot running movement and

Christopher McDougall's book, *Born to Run*.[16] The crux of the research shows that "barefoot runners who fore-foot strike generate smaller collision forces than shod rear-foot strikers."[17] This finding accords with the research cited above that also shatters the traditional assumption about the role supposedly played by an elevated cushioned heel in traditional running shoes. Instead of providing the shock absorption promised in running shoe advertising, elevated cushioned shoes can actually lead to greater impact forces with their false sense of security.[18]

K.G. Hatala and colleagues[19] support the finding by Lieberman's research team regarding the attenuation of impact forces with fore-foot landing; but also show that fore-foot landing is not a universal pattern among habitually barefoot populations. Rather, in the population they studied—the Daasanach of northern Kenya (Lieberman and colleagues studied Kalenjin runners in Kenya)—foot strike patterns varied with running speed. The Daasanach tended to switch to a mid-foot or fore-foot strike at faster speeds, a pattern more common to shod runners. In a panel discussion on barefoot running I attended a few years ago in Boulder, Olympic runner Alan Culpepper spoke to this pattern. He noted that he heel strikes on long, slow distance runs while he adopts a fore-foot strike at faster speeds and shorter distances.

Returning to the points made earlier,

whether the runner strikes first with the heel or the fore-foot appears to be less important than the amount of proprioception afforded the runner upon landing. The debate will continue over the pros and cons of different foot strike patterns; but we do know that increased proprioception allows for better diversion of impact forces. As running coach Bobby McGee explains in his video on running mechanics, "The more effectively the leg can load onto the surface, the less shock it needs to absorb, the more elastic energy it can store, and the more powerfully and economically it can return this power to the runner."[20]

Lessons from Habitually Barefoot Populations

Beyond the foot strike debate, there are additional (and more important) lessons to take from studying barefoot populations. As D'Aout and colleagues point out, habitually wearing shoes substantially alters foot shape and function.[21] Namely, unshod populations exhibit wider feet that more uniformly distribute peak pressures across the foot—which means more stability.

When walking or running barefoot, the toes splay out upon landing. Likewise, you also do this with your hands when, for example, you put them on the floor to do a push-up. However, the natural splaying of your toes is inhibited when wearing traditional shoes with a tapered toe box. The narrow toe box binds the toes together in the fore-foot. It's like a less extreme version of traditional Chinese foot binding.[22] Imagine trying to do daily tasks with the fingers of your hands bound together to prevent the individual digits from spreading out. Much dexterity, stability, and function is lost in the process.

Crucially, narrow shoes severely limit movement of the big toe. Why is this important? Because the big toe is responsible for providing nearly all your stability while running. In particular, the muscle known as the flexor hallucis brevis drives the foot down while the abductor hallucis widens the foot for improved leverage. As Dicharry notes, "If you can improve control to drive the big toe down and actively spread it, you'll experience true Zen in foot control."[23]

But effectively utilizing these muscles is impossible if your shoes bind your toes together. The bunions common among shod populations—which are unknown in barefoot populations—are a result of this form of modern day foot binding.

Setting aside the issue of footwear for a moment, I want to emphasize that all runners will benefit substantially from improving strength and neuromuscular control in the feet, especially the big toe. We target muscles throughout the legs, hip, abdominals and back to improve postural control and core stability. Why do that but neglect the intrinsic muscles of the feet which also contribute to stability? Unfortunately, this is what the traditional running shoe paradigm has encouraged us to do, pretending that PECH shoes can somehow magically replace the work otherwise required of the feet to absorb shock and provide stability.

But everything is connected up and down the body; and the feet need to work in conjunction with the legs and hips to run effectively. So in addition to strengthening your running core (with a focus on the glutes along with the stabilizing muscles of the hips), working the flexor hallucis brevis with "toe yoga" and big toe push-downs is equally important for staving off those traditional running injuries (e.g. shin splints, knee pain). Remember, this is as much about making your muscles "smarter" as it is making them stronger. Smarter, stronger feet will function more effectively to make you a more effective, less injury-prone runner.

In an effort to reverse the effects of modern day foot binding, Portland runner and podiatrist Dr. Ray McClanahan designed a product called Correct Toes. These simple yet effective toe spacers place each toe in an anatomical position more conducive to proper gait. Runners (or anyone who wears shoes regularly) will benefit greatly from their use. To a lesser extent, toe socks can be somewhat helpful in allowing your toes to separate and in avoiding restrictive constraints of tight socks.

Returning to the issue of shoes, the bottom line is that function is the name of the game. We want to choose shoes that encourage the foot to function normally. As D'Aout and colleagues emphasize, "footwear that fails to respect natural foot shape and function will ultimately alter the morphology and the biomechanical behavior of the foot." [24] Unfortunately, as just discussed, those alterations tend to be detrimental to our ability to run injury-free.

By providing the foot with necessary and needed room to function normally, a host of problems associated with shod runners can be reduced, including bunions, forefoot pain, shin splints, and knee pain.[25] We still have a lot to learn about the foot and its function by studying both shod and habitually unshod runners, but what we do know can help inform better choices for running shoe design.

It is important to emphasize here that the solution is not to simply ditch shoes entirely. Footwear provides definite protective advantages against hazards on the roads and trails. For runners who grow up in a habitually shod society, simply ditching shoes also has practical limitations. Plus, there is another issue to consider: running economy.

Running Economy

Running economy refers to how much oxygen (VO_2) a runner uses at a given pace. The less oxygen you need to run, say, a 6 minute mile, the more economical you are as a runner. Among the many variables that affect running economy is footwear. Heavier shoes means the runner carries more weight, and this requires more oxygen to maintain that 6 minute per mile pace. In fact, oxygen consumption increases by about 1 percent per 100 grams of weight added to shoes as studies have shown.[26]

Yet, as Jason Franz and colleagues[27] demonstrate in a study that compares barefoot versus shod running while controlling for weight (they placed small, weighted strips on the feet of barefoot runners to mimic the weight of shoes), shod running in lightweight shoes actually results in lower metabolic cost to the runner than barefoot running. The take-away point from their study is that *well-designed, lightweight shoes can actually be beneficial to running economy.*

What to Look for in Running Shoes

As ironic as it may sound, the barefoot running movement has resulted in greater choices of footwear for runners. Newer—especially "minimalist"—designs are heeding some of the lessons found in the research discussed above to provide better options to let the foot do what it needs to do to maximize proprioception and minimize impact forces.

In a nutshell, here is my advice on how to choose running shoes. Relative to your current footwear and situation, look for shoes that:

1. Minimize heel to toe drop

2. Minimize material under foot

3. Maximize room in the toe box

The aim is to reduce the barrier between your foot and the ground to enhance proprioception while still providing some cushion for protection and running economy. Shoe weight is another consideration (lighter being better), but moving away from severely elevated, cushioned heels generally results in automatic weight savings.

With regard to fit, remember that your toes need room to splay naturally during each foot plant while running. Add to this the fact that feet tend to spread out during the day (and during runs) as you accumulate time on feet. So try on shoes later in the day (or after a run), and leave about a finger's width between your toes and the end of the shoe. The shoe should also move with the foot rather than pulling away from it.

Proper width is crucial. Again, you want

enough room in the toe box to allow your toes to splay naturally, letting the flexor hallucis brevis (big toe) do its job without being constrained.

A good test to see if the shoes you are considering provide enough room in the forefoot is to take out the insole and place it on the ground. Now stand on the insole barefoot. If your fore-foot and toes extend beyond the sides of the insole, this means your foot is going to be squeezed every time you take a step while running (just like in the x-ray photo above). This is what is meant by modern day foot binding! This is a clear sign the shoe is not for you. Look for one with a roomier toe box to better fit the width of your forefoot while standing. Sometimes this can be achieved by ordering a wider width.

Finally, note that I say these three maxims should be implemented relative to your current footwear and situation. Everyone starts in a different place with different needs and readiness for change. Switching directly from a motion-control shoe with a high heel to a minimalist shoe with no heel will introduce its own separate issues if done too soon and too quickly. One can still heed the maxims (especially the third one) without going completely minimalist. But any move toward more (relatively speaking) minimalist footwear is best achieved by taking a gradual approach.

The best place to start as you as you

implement the maxims above isn't with the shoes at all. It's with a few simple exercises and drills to increase the strength and proprioception in your feet. Keep in mind that as your feet get stronger, muscles develop at a faster rate than bones, tendons (i.e. muscle to bone attachments), and ligaments (i.e. bone to bone attachments). This is especially important to keep in mind if you want to move toward truly minimalist shoes or even try barefoot running.

Again, introduce any radical changes to your footwear gradually. Start with a few minutes during one of your weekly runs. Build up to one run a week. Then add another run each week. And so on. This is a good way to progress not only for those moving toward more minimalist shoes, but for those wishing to do some barefoot running.

Even shod runners can benefit from small amounts of barefoot running, such as a lap around the grass on the inside of a track during a cool down or a few barefoot striders on a grassy field. There is nothing more enjoyable than running when your feet are free to function naturally—whether barefoot or in properly designed shoes.

Find good shoes that allow your feet to function well and you will experience more joy and longevity as a runner.

ADEQUATE WIDTH IS KEY TO RUNNING SHOE FIT

When assessing the fit of new running shoes, it is important that you fit shoes to your feet rather than trying to fit your feet to the shoes. One of the most important (and overlooked) elements to look for is adequate width in the toebox, which is vital for your foot's ability to function properly while running.

When you stand, walk or run barefoot, your toes splay out to provide stability. Shoes with a tapered toebox inhibit this spreading of the toes, and instead bind the toes together. This squeezing of the forefoot by a tapered toebox has been likened to a modern day version of foot binding. As a result, much foot function is lost.

In particular, when your toes are

constrained in a narrow toebox, your big toe is pushed inward and loses its ability to support the foot. The result is less stability. Issues from bunions to shin splints can eventually result.

The solution to avoiding these problems is simple. Find shoes that allow adequate room in the forefoot so your toes can splay naturally while standing, walking and running. Here's how.

Remove the insole from the shoes and stand on the insole barefoot while allowing your toes to spread naturally. If the width of your foot extends beyond the edges of the insole, there is not enough room in the toebox to allow your foot to function properly.

Keep searching until you find shoes that fit your feet. Don't simply squeeze your feet into shoes that are too narrow and sacrifice foot function. Fortunately, more running shoes are being made with wider toeboxes to allow for the natural splaying of the toes. A newer shoe company called Altra is one, and New Balance does a nice job on some of their minimalist models. Many choices exist and it's important to find one that works for you.

Once you've found shoes with adequate width in the toebox, next work on improving dexterity in your big toe by incorporating a few minutes of "toe yoga" into your daily activities (move your big toe separately from your other toes). The goal is to improve your ability to drive down and spread the big toe for improved leverage and control while running. Paying attention to these elements of running shoe choice and toe mobility will pay dividends by helping you run injury-free.

EASY GUIDELINES FOR CHOOSING RUNNING SHOES

Relative to what you are currently using, look for shoes that:

1. Minimize heel to toe drop

2. Minimize material under foot

3. Maximize room in the toe box

The aim is to reduce the barrier between your foot and the ground to enhance proprioception while still providing some cushion for protection and running economy.

A good fit requires adequate length and width to allow your toes to splay naturally while running. In addition, you want a shoe that moves with the foot rather than pulling away from it.

To Check Length

While standing in the shoes, there should be about a thumb's width between your toes and the end of the shoe.

To Check Width

Take out the insole of the shoe and place it on the ground. Stand on the insole barefoot. If your fore-foot and toes extend beyond the sides of the insole, they are not wide enough. Look for shoes with a roomier toe box to better fit the width of your forefoot while standing. Sometimes this can be achieved by ordering a wider width.

When to Try on Shoes

Feet spread out during the day (and during runs) as you accumulate time on feet. So try on shoes later in the day (or after a run).

Basic Running Gear Every Runner Should Own

The sport of running is about as simple as you can get, requiring very little equipment to get started. Whether you are a new runner or a young runner about to join your high school cross country team, here is an overview of the basic items you will need to get the most out of your running.

Shoes

Foot structures vary and so do a runner's shoe needs. But the most important thing to keep in mind is to find as minimal a shoe as necessary to meet your needs. This means as lightweight a shoe as possible with the smallest amount of heel to toe drop you are comfortable with and only as much pronation control as you truly need (if you've never used a shoe with pronation control and have never had any related injuries, there is no need to start wearing that type of shoe).

Also, be sure the toe box in your shoes provides enough room for your toes to spread while standing. To find out, take out the insole and place it on the ground. Now stand on the insole. If your forefoot and toes extend beyond the sides of the insole, this means your foot is going to be squeezed every time you take a step while running. This is a clear sign the shoe is not for you. Look for one with a roomier toe box.

Socks

Since we're on the topic of shoes, it's probably a good idea to mention something about socks. Choose running socks that are made of a moisture wicking material. This typically means a synthetic material (although smart wool is also popular among some runners). Definitely avoid cotton. Thin socks tend to work best. If you have blister problems, then two layers of thin socks work much better than a single thick sock. But if you double up your socks, make sure you choose your running shoe size with that in mind.

Warmups

Even if you live in a warmer climate, you

should own at least one pair of running pants and a running jacket. This can be as simple as a pair of sweat pants and a cotton sweatshirt, although technical materials will be much more comfortable once you start sweating in them (or running in the rain). And you should be prepared to sweat in your warmups. After all, the point is to use them to help you warm up prior to workouts and races so you aren't starting off cold. If it is below 65 degrees when you start out, wear them until you are warmed up.

Clothing

Since I've mentioned "moisture wicking" and "technical" materials a few times now, it is probably worth making a few more notes in this area. In both colder and hotter temperatures, technical materials that are designed to pull moisture away from your skin will keep you more comfortable. They will keep you cooler on hot days and warmer on cold days.

The main thing with clothing is to find items that are comfortable for you. As *Homo sapiens*, we rely upon clothing to help adjust to the environment around us. It is a good idea to learn how to make the most of clothing options to stay cool on hot days and warm on cold days. At the least, this means wearing your warmups to workouts/races when it is below 65 degrees, and being ready to put on dry clothes and warmups after completing your workouts/races in cooler weather.

Wristwatch

I consider a basic running watch to be just as essential as a good pair of running shoes for a serious runner. Why? Because as a competitive runner you need to become more aware of your times while running. And the best way to do this is to wear and use a watch with a stopwatch function. This will allow you to monitor the duration of runs prescribed by your coach. During interval sessions, it will allow you to keep track of your interval times. And it will help you monitor your pace during runs of known distances. Tuning into time will help you become a better and more aware runner.

There you have it. Those are the basic items any new runner should own. There is beauty in the simplicity of running. With running, it's amazing how a minimal amount of gear can bring about a maximal amount of enjoyment once you get out there and run.

Dressing for Winter Running

Unless you're vacationing on a tropical beach, the chill of winter can sometimes present a challenge to training as usual. But as long as you are prepared—and dress the part—winter can be an incredibly rewarding time of the year to train outside. Here are a few tips on how to dress appropriately for winter training.

Despite cooler temperatures, the body still sweats when exercising in cold weather. And highly trained athletes are especially adept at triggering the sweat mechanism. The key to dealing with sweat during cold weather training is to wear layers of technical materials.

Technical materials wick the moisture away from the skin, keeping you drier and warmer as the intensity heats up. There are many synthetic materials that do the job, including polypropylene, nylon, polyester, spandex, and various blends. In addition, wool is an excellent natural material.

But stay away from cotton. The same reason you want cotton in your bath towel is the same reason you want to avoid it while working out. Cotton excels at absorbing water and sweat. There's nothing worse than a layer of cold sweat trapped next to your body while exercising outside during winter.

Once you've chosen appropriate materials, the next step is to dress in layers. This means wearing a few layers of lighter weight items, rather than a single thick one. When you first step outside, you will need more warmth until you are into the workout. But once you get going (or as the weather changes), you want the ability to remove or add layers to regulate your temperature.

Start with a lightweight, breathable base layer. End with an outer layer appropriate to the conditions. If it is windy, wear a jacket with some wind protection. If it is rainy or snowy, wear a jacket that provides wetness protection. If it is calm and sunny, opt for a more breathable outer layer such as fleece or wool or another cold weather shirt to wear over your bottom layer.

Protect the head and neck. A great deal of heat escapes from these areas of the body.

Choose a hat or headband made of technical materials to keep the warmth in and wick away the sweat. A hat that covers the top of the head will be warmer than a headband that merely wraps around the ears. A turtleneck or neck gaiter can keep the neck extra warm. In really cold weather, a balaclava provides extra coverage for the face.

The extremities—feet and hands—are especially prone to cold. As body temperature drops, blood from the extremities is shunted to the core. This can shield against oncoming hypothermia (low internal body temperature) but can leave the extremities susceptible to frostnip (skin numbness or tingling due to cold) or frostbite (damage due to freezing skin).

For the hands, be sure to wear gloves or mittens that provide appropriate insulation. I always keep around several basic pairs of running gloves since I go through them like socks in the winter. I especially like lightweight gloves with grips on the palms for dexterity.

For the feet, keep in mind the points about technical materials made earlier. Avoid cotton. Use synthetic materials or smart wool to wick away moisture and provide insulation. It is usually best to stick with the same thickness of sock you normally wear with your shoes. But you can wear longer versions of that sock to ensure ankle coverage. I especially like to wear compression socks or sleeves to keep my ankles and calves warm during winter training.

For running as well as snowshoeing, sometimes a larger pair of cycling booties or shoe covers can be used over the top of running shoes if you will be moving through deep snow. Another option is to take a plastic bag and wear this between your socks and shoes. This provides a cheap layer of protection against the elements to keep your feet warm. If you want to get more sophisticated, look for vapor barrier or waterproof socks such as SealSkinz.

Last but not least, don't forget the under layer. Remember the rule about cotton. Leave the cotton undies for casual, non-perspiring activities. There are plenty of technical fabric options that wick away moisture while providing support, comfort and warmth.

The trick to staying warm in winter training is preparation. Once you have the appropriate materials, then dress in layers and add/remove items as the conditions warrant. When well equipped, there can be nothing more exhilarating than a good workout outdoors during the winter months.

NUTRITION AND HYDRATION FOR TRAINING AND RECOVERY

Just as sleep is a vital component of effective recovery, so is a healthy diet. When it comes to eating well, it may be worth emphasizing in today's world of fast food and highly processed comestibles that the best sources of nutrition are whole foods with minimal processing rather than pre-packaged meals and snack items. Eating a wide variety of whole foods, and satisfying cravings within reason, ensures you are getting the nutrients you need to stay fueled and healthy.

In terms of macro-nutrients (carbohydrates, proteins, fats), athletes typically require 5-19 grams of carbohydrate per kilogram of body weight, 1.2-2 grams of protein per kilogram of body weight, and 0.8-3.0 grams of fat per kilogram of body weight. The exact amounts vary according to the training phase and amount of training you are engaged in. Enough water and fluids should be consumed so that your urine is the color of straw.

Beyond basic dietary guidelines, a few tips should be kept in mind to enhance post-workout recovery. In exercise bouts that last over 60-90 minutes, muscle glycogen (the body's carbohydrate stores) become depleted and needs to be replaced. It is best to start this process within a half hour (or at least within an hour) after exercise by consuming around 0.5 grams of carbohydrate per pound of body weight. For example, a 160 pound runner would target about 80 grams of carbohydrate, which translates into a snack of 320 calories (e.g. a couple of bananas and a bagel). Your choice of snack will depend upon your personal preferences, but this is not the time to pig out on cookies or ice cream. Keep the snack healthy and you will start your recovery on the right track.

One of the body's reactions to intense exercise is inflammation. Reducing inflammation is therefore an important part of the recovery process. Essential fatty acids help to decrease the body's inflammation response, and should be an important part of the athlete's daily diet. In particular, the omega-3 fatty acid is often underrepresented in typical diets. Cold water fish (e.g. tuna, salmon) and flax seeds/oil are excellent sources of omega-3. Yet another food item that has anti-inflammatory properties is pineapple—specifically, the enzyme bromelain that is found in pineapple. Instead of reaching for a soda, try a glass of cold pineapple juice instead. It also provides a nice dose of carbohydrates to help replenish depleted glycogen stores in the muscles.

LONG RUN HYDRATION LOGISTICS

Figuring out how to stay hydrated and fueled during long runs always seems to be a challenge. Below are the pros and cons of a few long run hydration strategies. Experimentation is the key to finding the strategy or strategies that work best for you given the type of run, terrain and weather conditions.

Multiple Loops around an "Aid Station"

This solution tends to work best if you can find a route of about 3 to 5 miles that loops around a trailhead or parking lot. Keep a cooler with sport drink and energy bars in the car. Make sure the supplies are laid out and easily accessible so that you can quickly grab what you need after each loop of the run. This solution seems to be the easiest without requiring you to carry anything as you run—and in that regard, it mimics race day conditions where you are allowed to focus simply on running.

A drawback of this solution is that it might be difficult to find a route of an appropriate distance. A long loop is great for mixing up the scenery and terrain, but leaves you without frequent aid. On the other hand, a short loop provides frequent aid but can get a bit monotonous. Aim for a route that will allow you to pass by the "aid station" every half hour—more or less depending upon weather conditions and personal needs.

Pre-positioning Aid along the Route

Like the multiple loops around an "aid station" strategy, this solution also frees you from needing to carry anything along the route, which again mimics race day conditions. Prior to the run, stash water bottles along the route while biking or driving the course. Instead of being tied to a single loop, this strategy affords you a greater home range over which to travel during the long run. Plus, you can leave aid exactly where you want/need it, such as placing more aid over the last half of the run. However, more time is required pre- and post-run to deal with the logistics.

Be sure to mark and remember well the "aid station" locations; and don't litter! Be responsible with any empty water bottles you leave along the way—stash them as strategically as you stashed the full ones and return to pick them up after the run.

Using a Hydration Pack

To best ensure you are never far from water during a long run, simply carry it with you. While in the past, the choices runners had in this regard were limited and ill-conceived, now there are more choices than ever. A host of companies—including CamelBak, Fuel Belt, Ultimate Direction, Nathan, Salomon and GoLite—offer a wide range of hydration packs that are designed specifically to conform to the jostling demands of running. Different types of packs may be better or worse depending upon the type of course and length/speed of the run you are doing. Here's an overview of the main options.

Waist Packs

In my experience, waist packs tend to be the least cumbersome while running. Obviously, the smaller the water bottles (and the less you carry), the more you are able to mimic running *sans* pack.

In that regard, I like the Fuel Belt Endurance—with its four 8-ounce flasks distributed equally around the waist (plus a pocket for a few gels)—for faster paced long runs on tamer terrain. Products of this type let you to carry 16 to 32 ounces of water/sport drink (you can leave out two of the water bottles for shorter runs) along with a few gels or an energy bar while still allowing you to open up your stride and run at a fairly decent pace without jostling.

In addition, since there are multiple water bottles balanced on both side of your hips, you can alternate the bottles you drink from to more or less maintain the weight distribution throughout the run. Multiple small bottles also allow you to carry different types of liquid so you can have both water to wash down gels and sport drink to use on its own.

If you wish to carry more in a waist pack, look for ones that provide a holster or two for standard size bike bottles along with a zippered pocket and/or lash cords to stash a jacket. Products like the Salomon Twin Belt, for example, allow you to carry two 20-ounce water bottles, energy gels, plus a jacket or hat. The dual water bottles are ideal for maintaining a more or less equal weight distribution so as not to throw off your stride while running.

Backpacks

For long trail runs, sometimes a lightweight hydration backpack is the best option. These packs typically include a bladder with a tube/straw à la the original CamelBak systems. The bladders can hold one to two liters of water or sport drink.

I especially find this option useful on long trail runs where I know I'll be out for hours moving at a much slower pace than if I were on tamer terrain. The slower pace and verticality of mountain trails typically makes jostling less of an issue. Running backpacks also provide you with more room to stash trail mix and extra clothes for changing weather conditions.

The Nathan Hydration Vest works well in this regard. It is remarkably stable while running even when you have the two liter bladder filled. One drawback, however, is that the two pockets on the front of the vest sit right in the path of where a runner's hands swing. I found this annoying if I put more than a gel or two in these front pockets. This made the front pockets more or less useless and required stashing more food in the rear of the pack, which inevitably takes away ever-so-slightly from the stability of the pack when it is full.

For long mountain trail runs, I also like the Go-Lite Rush. This is closer to a lightweight rucksack than a running pack, but it does work well for long trail runs in the mountains. The pack includes a sleeve for a two liter bladder, plus enough volume to stash plenty of food, clothes and even a water filter if you will be out for several hours and need to refill at a stream. It also features a waist belt with pockets. The waist belt helps to keep the pack in place, and the small pockets integrated into the belt are ideal for quick access to bars or gels. Plus, unlike the higher positioned pockets on the Nathan Hydration Vest, these pockets don't get in the way of your arm swing while running. The drawback of the Go-Lite Rush is that it can jostle a bit if you pick up the pace, especially on fast descents.

Hand Held Water Bottles

For those who don't like strapping a pack to their waist or back, another option includes hand held water bottles. These systems consist of a fabric cradle attached to a water bottle— your hand slips into the cradle and allows you to hold the water bottle with very little effort. The cradle also provides a small pocket for stashing a few gels or an energy bar.

Although many of these devices are designed to hold standard 20-ounce water bottles, I personally find that too bulky. Moreover, given that it's a good idea to evenly distribute any extra weight you carry while running so as not throw off your stride, it makes sense to opt for two smaller hand held carriers instead of one big one. In this regard, the Ultimate Direction 10-ounce Fast Draw works well.

However, keep in mind that carrying two hand held water bottles eliminates the use of your hands—both hands! I didn't realize how much I used my hands during a long run—to wipe sweat from my eyes, to adjust my hat, to open gels, to swat bugs, etc.—until I did a long run with two hand held water bottles.

My own preference for carrying water during long runs lies with the waist packs or backpacks. For faster paced runs on tamer terrain, I prefer a lightweight waist pack. For slower paced runs on mountain trails with lots of verticality, I prefer a lightweight backpack. Weigh the pros and cons of the different options against your own needs to find the best hydration strategy for your long runs.

Tuning into Heart Rate to Prevent Overtraining

Understanding how to balance training and recovery is key to any athlete's success. As an athlete, you need to work hard to achieve fitness gains but not so hard as to end up in the dreaded overtraining zone.

Once you've dug yourself into a hole with overtraining, it may take several weeks to climb out; and extreme cases can be season ending. So overtraining is obviously to be avoided.

Here are a few tips on how to use heart rate to read the signs. By tuning into your heart rate, you can gain a window into your state of recovery so you have a better idea when to push it or when to back off in your training.

Inability to Elevate Heart Rate during Training

One sign that you may need another recovery workout instead of that planned high intensity workout is how your heart rate responds during a training session.

Let's say you are pushing the envelope with hard training and enter into a workout knowing you're close to the edge of overreaching. After you do your initial warmup you dive into a set of intervals at a higher intensity level. Although a bit sluggish at first, you seem to be close to the target according to your pace. However, you are unable to elevate your heart rate into the target zone, a fact confirmed by your heart rate monitor.

In this case, an inability to elevate your heart rate when you've clearly upped the intensity indicates your body has not recovered from previous sessions. Heed the sign and turn that interval session into a short recovery workout. Then go home and conscientiously facilitate further recovery over the next few days before returning to higher intensity training.

Elevated Morning Heart Rate

Ideally, we would like a way to determine how recovered we are before even starting a workout. This is where morning heart rate readings can prove instructive.

A simple approach is to take your heart rate each morning before getting out of bed. Keep track of the average over time. If your heart rate is 5 to 10 beats higher than average on a given morning, this is a sign you may need more rest and recovery that day. It could also mean your body is fighting an oncoming virus, in which case eliminating stress in the form of hard training can give your body a chance to nip any sort of oncoming illness in the bud.

Elevated Orthostatic Heart Rate

Another variation of the resting heart rate test is to take your orthostatic heart rate. You can do this in the morning before getting out of bed or after lying down and resting for at least 15 minutes.

Start by taking your resting heart rate while lying down. Next, stand up and take your heart rate. Subtract the difference between the lying and standing readings. If the difference is more than 15 to 20 beats; then additional recovery is called for.

These simple techniques can provide measurable insight into your state of recovery. The more experience you gain in using these techniques, the better you will be able to read the nuanced signs of overtraining. Remember, performance gains are attained in between workout sessions when your body adapts. Recovery is essential to this process.

How to Facilitate Recovery

Everyone knows that improving athletic performance requires putting in the requisite amount of work during training sessions.

Yet given the propensity for type-A athletes to pile on as much training as possible in the quest for greater performance gains, the flip side of the training equation can easily be neglected.

In short, it is important to remember that the effects of training are not gained during a training session itself but during the recovery periods between sessions.

Given that recovery is an integral part of the training equation, here are some tips that can help you speed your recovery from those hard training and racing days.

Cool Down Thoroughly

Your recovery begins the minute you have completed the last work interval during your hard training session. High intensity activity leads to the accumulation of lactic acid in the bloodstream, which can lead to that heavy muscle feeling. The easiest way to begin clearing away blood lactate is to run at an easy pace at the end of your workout. Low level aerobic activity turns that lactate into energy and removes it from the muscles.

Active Recovery on Days Off

Although sometimes a day spent lying on the couch and napping is just what the body needs, on many "rest days" the body will benefit from some type of activity. Walks, yoga or other light activity that gets the body moving stimulates the lymph and circulatory systems, which are important to the recovery process. The key is to keep the activity easy. If you choose to do a light run or cross-training on a "rest day," then limit that session to a short, easy warm up—just enough to raise the body temperature, produce a bit of sweat and get the blood flowing.

Take the Cold Water Plunge

Jumping in a cold bath or even taking a

cold shower can help reduce muscle soreness following intense exercise. By increasing circulation, cold plunges can speed the removal of toxins associated with muscle damage. Even a plunge of only 30 to 45 seconds can have a benefit. If you don't have access to a cold mountain stream or an ice bath; then set the faucet to 'cold' for the last few minutes of your shower. Especially during the warm summer months, there's nothing more refreshing than a cold shower after a tough workout.

Sports Massage

Flush out the muscles with a light sports massage. Deep tissue work has its place in the recovery cycle, but nothing beats a light flush of the muscles so that you can get back to it with fresher legs the next day. Like a cold water plunge, sports massage can help push out the toxins from a hard exercise bout. Even ten minutes on your own with a massage stick can be beneficial.

Compression Sleeves

By now you should have noticed a theme. Things that aid blood circulation help recovery. Add the new fad of compression sleeves to that list. It is no mystery why the medical field has long been using compression garments with surgery patients before athletes discovered them. Wearing compression socks/sleeves can improve venous return from those hammered calves. While the jury is still out on whether wearing them during training/racing can help performance, they certainly do have positive benefits for aiding recovery between workouts.

EFAs

One of the body's reactions to intense exercise is inflammation. Reducing inflammation is therefore an important part of the recovery process. Essential fatty acids help to decrease the body's inflammation response, and should be an important part of the athlete's daily diet. In particular, the omega-3 fatty acid is often underrepresented in typical diets. Cold water fish (e.g. tuna, salmon) and flax seeds/oil are excellent sources of omega-3.

Pineapple Juice

Yet another food item that has anti-inflammatory properties is pineapple—specifically, the enzyme bromelain that is found in pineapple. Instead of reaching for a soda, try a glass of cold pineapple juice instead. It also provides a nice dose of carbohydrates to help replenish depleted glycogen stores in the muscles.

Remember, fitness gains occur during recovery. A proper recovery allows your body a chance to adapt from a hard training session, and will ensure that it is ready to get the most out of the next one.

STAY HEALTHY WITH PREVENTIVE SELF-MASSAGE

One of the easiest and most effective means to ensure the healthy rebuilding of the body in between workouts is to use self-massage techniques. All you need is a few minutes each day along with some useful tools that include a foam roller, rolling stick, lacrosse ball, and golf ball.

Why Tissue Maintenance is Important

Collagen is a protein found in connective tissues in the body. And connective tissues are found everywhere, including the tendons that connect muscles to bones, the fasciae that surround muscle groups, and the endomysium that surrounds individual muscle cells.

When collagen fibers run parallel, like straws in a box, everything works the way it should. Muscles can contract without obstructions and tissues are able to withstand the stress loads placed upon them through physical activity. But the simple fact is that training breaks down the body. If it didn't, there would be no opportunity to grow stronger through positive adaptations during the rebuilding phase.

As long as the tissues heal properly, then mobility is maintained and the body can continue to function at a high level of performance. But complete tissue rebuilding can take up to a few weeks while training takes place on an ongoing basis. That means there are ample opportunities for tissues to rebuild in a less than effective manner. Instead of the collagen fibers lining up in parallel like straws in a box, the fibers begin to look more like a pile of straws arranged in a haphazard fashion. This is when adhesions, scars or trigger points begin to develop. The key to ensuring healthy tissues is to be proactive with self-massage.

How to Maintain Healthy Tissues

The key to ensuring healthy tissues is to dedicate a few minutes each day to preventive care. A daily check-in with your body will keep the tissues healthy and allow you to notice trigger points when they first begin to develop so you can eliminate them before they get worse. This preventive tissue work is made easy with a few readily available tools.

The first tool is a foam roller, which is a cylinder made of dense foam. Foam rollers are about 5-6 inches in diameter and a foot or more in length. A foam roller works well for targeting larger areas, such as the back, quads, hamstrings, calves, and the IT band.

Complementary to the foam roller is a rolling massage stick, which can make it easy to target certain areas, such as the calves, the front of the lower leg, the neck, IT band, quads and hamstrings.

For smaller areas on the body where more targeted pressure is needed, a lacrosse ball is the tool of choice. The lacrosse ball can be used pinpoint trigger points or trouble spots, such as in the lower back, buttocks or hips.

And a golf ball is indispensable for the bottom of the feet to keep the plantar fasciae healthy and happy. And it also can be used to strengthen the muscles in the feet as you grip it, pick it up and move it around.

Some a few minutes each day with these tools to keep your body moving for optimal performance.

Are You Sleeping Enough?

The recommended amount of sleep for healthy adults is 7-9 hours per day. According to the Centers for Disease Control (CDC),[28] 30 percent of American adults are "sleep deprived," meaning they sleep less than 6 hours each day—leaving them vulnerable to adverse health and safety effects.

As any athlete in training knows, skipping on sleep is not conducive to optimal athletic performance. Train as much as you want, but without adequate sleep the body is unable to absorb the training. That is because physiological adaptations occur during the recovery periods in between training bouts. Without rest and recovery, the body continues to break down rather than to rebuild.

Athletes in training should aim for the recommended 7-9 hours of sleep each day plus additional hours depending upon their activity level. Here are a few rules of thumb for determining how much extra sleep to include in your weekly schedule.

Rule of Thumb #1

A good general rule of thumb is to take the number of hours you train each week, move the decimal point one place to the left, and add that amount of time to your daily sleep. For example, if you train for 10 hours a week; then aim for an extra hour of sleep each day. If you normally find yourself needing 8 hours of sleep; then you would bump that up to 9 hours.

Rule of Thumb #2

Another general rule is to take the number of miles you run per week and aim for the same number of extra minutes of sleep per night. For example, if you run 30 miles per week in your training; then aim for an extra 30 minutes per day of sleep. If you normally find yourself needing 7½ hours of sleep per night; then you would bump that up to 8 hours.

To be sure, these are simply rules of thumb, and you will need to pinpoint your own particular needs based on individual circumstances. But they do help to underscore the key take-away point: *You will need more sleep than you are used to during heavy training periods.*

At the minimum, make sure you get the recommended baseline of 7-9 hours per day; then add in extra time according to your activity level and individual needs. If you're training 20 hours a week; then sleeping 10 hours a day is not a luxury—it's a necessity.

Keep in mind, extra sleep need not occur only at night. Naps during the day, particularly after intense workouts, are another good way to ensure you get the rest you need.

At the very least, dedicate that extra time to rest and relaxation even if it's not a full sleep. Your body will thank you and you will put yourself in a position to feel better both on and off the race course.

Today's Workout is a Nap

If you're like most endurance athletes, the idea of a nap for a workout not only sounds oxymoronic but downright blasphemous. After all, the definition of a workout is "a session of vigorous physical exercise." And a period of slumber is anything but a session of vigorous physical exercise. But, then again, that is the entire point.

As we know from Exercise Physiology 101, the training process involves a stimulus that triggers a physiological response in the body which results in a positive adaptation (a fitness gain). Notably, the positive adaptation occurs after the stimulus breaks the body down a bit and has a chance to rebuild. In rebuilding to better handle such stimuli again (such as running several miles at a fast rate of speed), the body benefits from a positive training effect that leads to an improved state of fitness.

In other words, the basic equation that underlies training looks like this:

$$Training + Recovery = Fitness$$

As athletes, we focus intently on the "training" part of this equation. After all, hard work is the *sine qua non* for building fitness and improving performance. So we engage in "sessions of vigorous physical exercise" (otherwise known as workouts or training sessions), attempting to provide the necessary overload appropriate to our individual situation and thereby grow stronger and become faster.

Yet problems arise when the other part of that training equation is neglected: *recovery*. When you wake up at 6 am to go to the track to do those cruise intervals, get to the office by 8 am for an eight hour day of work, take a break at lunch for some strength training, and then squeeze in a recovery run in the evening, there is little time left in the day to dedicate specifically to recovery.

Sure, it may be possible to handle this type of training schedule day in and day out with little sleep...if you're young, have a low stress job or are gifted with the genes of an Olympic caliber athlete (and even then everyone must pay homage to the full equation of the training process one way or another). But if you're like the rest of the active population that engage in endurance events while juggling work, family, school and other life commitments, consistently neglecting the recovery part of the training equation can take a toll—not just on your athletic performance, but on your ability to enjoy life to the fullest.

It's not normal to walk around like a zombie tired all the time from hard training and stressful work. If that sounds like you, the solution is to pay specific attention to your recovery in your training plan. I'll go as far as to say that you should pay as much attention to your recovery as you do to your training schedule. So how is that to be accomplished in a sport that lauds killer workouts and the ability to squeeze training out of every waking minute not spent at the office or with family?

Try this. When you put together your upcoming training week, specifically schedule in "workouts" dedicated to, yes, taking a nap, or some other form of recovery activity, such as spending an hour in your Recovery Boots reading a book. And here's the clincher (I know this is hard for some of you): when you see this nap or rest time on your schedule, you must treat it as seriously as any key workout that week. Coach's orders!

If you are a constantly-on-the-go athlete, this strategy can help you adhere to both sides of the full training equation, while taking the guilt out of using a perfectly good hour of the day for a nap. After all, if it's on the training schedule it will be easier to hold yourself accountable to this necessary—yet often neglected—aspect of the training process.

APPENDIX

Training Intensity Zones

Training zones are the target ranges of heart rate or pace used to prescribe workout intensities. They are specific to the activity, so you will have different training zones for each discipline in which you train.

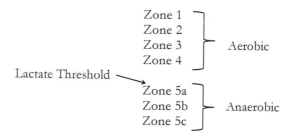

Training zones for characterizing exercise intensity

ADAM HODGES

The first four zones correspond to aerobic
intensity levels. The last three zones fall within
the anaerobic range. The lactate threshold (LT)
falls right between Zone 4 and Zone 5a, acting
as the boundary between aerobic and anaerobic
intensity.

Of the four aerobic zones, Zone 1 is used
primarily for recovery and warmup or
warmdown efforts. Zone 2 is the primary
aerobic base building zone. It can also be
thought of as "conversational" pace, meaning
you can still talk with a training partner while
running at this pace. This is the zone for long
runs—popularly referred to as long slow
distance (LSD).

Zone 3 represents a more challenging
aerobic pace. It's still well within the aerobic
range but involves a peppier tempo that can be
hard for the uninitiated or untrained. Working
in this zone is a stepping stone to tempo work
that is closer to the lactate threshold. It is used
sparingly, but can play a role during base
training to prepare the body for higher intensity
lactate threshold sessions to come.

Zone 4 moves toward the lactate threshold
but remains sub-threshold. This is the
"comfortably hard" effort that runners refer to
when talking about tempo runs.

The lactate threshold arrives at the bottom
of Zone 5a, so Zone 5a corresponds to the
super-threshold range. The sub- and super-

threshold zones represent an important range that targets increases in the LT. Tempo workouts and cruise intervals in Zones 4-5a improve lactate tolerance and decrease lactate accumulation, which enhances the ability to sustain race pace.

Zone 5b is the next step up in the anaerobic range. This range typically corresponds to the athlete's maximal oxygen consumption, or VO_2max. Working in this zone expands aerobic capacity and enhances anaerobic endurance, or the ability to work anaerobically for events or portions of events that last a few minutes in length—such as the 800m or 1500m track events, the start or finish of a race, hard climbs, etc.

Finally, Zone 5c emphasizes anaerobic power. Work in this zone targets the ability to maintain short durations of speed (starts, race surges, finishing kicks).

ADAM HODGES

Notes & References

[1] See the appendix for an explanation of training zones.

[2] See the appendix for an explanation of training zones.

[3] See the appendix for an explanation of training zones.

[4] Woods, Krista; Phillip Bishop; and Eric Jones. 2009. "Warmu-Up and Stretching in the Prevention of Muscular Injury." *Sports Medicine* 37(12): 1089-1099.

[5] Katzmarzyk, Peter T.; Church, Timothy S.; Craig, Cora L.; and Bouchard, Claude. 2009. "Sitting Time and Mortality from All Causes, Cardiovascular Disease, and Cancer." *Medicine & Science in Sports & Exercise* 41(5): 998-1005.

Owen, N., Bauman, A. and Brown, W. 2009. "Too Much Sitting: A Novel and Important Predictor of Chronic Disease Risk?" *British Journal of Sports Medicine* 43(2): 81-83.

Roy, Brad A. 2012. "Sit Less and Stand and Move More." *ACSM's Health and Fitness Journal* 16(2): 4.

[6] Hamilton, Marc T.; Healy, Genevieve N.; Dunstan, David W.; Zderic, Theodore W.; and Owen, Neville. 2008. "Too Little Exercise and Too much Sitting: Inactivity Physiology and the Need for New Recommendations on Sedentary Behavior." *Current Cardiovascular Risk Reports* 2(4): 292-298.

[7] Cichanowski, H. R.; Schmitt, J. S.; Johnson, R. J.; Niemuth, P. E. 2007. "Hip Strength in Collegiate Female Athletes with Patellofemoral Pain." *Medicine & Science in Sports & Exercise* 39(8): 1227-1232.

Fredericson, M.; Cookingham, C. L.; Chaudhari, A. M.; Dowdell, B. C.; Oestreicher, N.; Sahrmann, S. A. 2000. "Hip Abductor Weakness in Distance Runners with Iliotibial Band Syndrome." *Clinical Journal of Sports Medicine* 10(11): 169-175.

Ireland, M. L.; Willson, J. D.; Ballantyne, B. T.; Davis, I. S. 2003. "Hip Strength in Females With and Without Patellofemoral Pain." *Journal of Orthopaedic & Sports Physical Therapy* 33 (11): 671-676.

Niemuth, P. E.; Johnson, R. J.; Myers, M. J.; Thieman, T. J. 2005. "Hip Muscle Weakness and Overuse Injuries in Recreational Runners." *Clinical Journal of Sports Medicine* 15(1): 14-21.

[8] Richards, Craig E., Parker J. Magin, and Robin Callister. 2009. "Is Your Prescription of Distance Running Shoes Evidence Based?" *British Journal of Sports Medicine* 43(3): 159-162.

[9] Knapik, J.J., D.W. Trone, D.I. Swedler, A. Villasenor, S.H. Bullock, E. Schmied, T. Bockelman, P. Han, and

B.H. Jones. 2010. "Injury Reduction Effectiveness of Assigning Running Shoes Based on Plantar Shape in Marine Corps Basic Training." *American Journal of Sports Medicine* 38(9): 1759-67.

[10] Dicharry, Jay, Jason R. Franz, Ugo Della Croce, Robert P. Wilder, Patrick O. Riley, D. Casey Kerrigan. 2009. "Differences in Static and Dynamic Measures in Evaluation of Talonavicular Mobility in Gait." *Journal of Orthopaedic and Sports Physical Therapy* 39(8): 628-634.

[11] Barnes, A., J. Wheat, and C. Milner. 2008. "Association between Foot Type and Tibial Stress Injuries: A Systematic Review." *British Journal of Sports Medicine* 42(2): 93-8.

Barnes, A., J. Wheat, and C. Milner. 2011. "Fore- and Rearfoot Kinematics in High- and Low-arched Individuals during Running." *Foot & Ankle International* 32(7): 710-6.

[12] Hennig, E.M., A. Gordon, Q. Liu. 1996. "Biomechanical Variables and the Perception of Cushioning for Running in Various Types of Footwear." *Journal of Applied Biomechanics* 12(2): 143-150.

Lake, M.J., and M.A. Lafortune. 1998. "Mechanical Inputs Related to Perception of Lower Extremity Impact Loading Severity." *Medicine & Science in Sports & Exercise* 30(1): 136-143.

Robbins, Steven E. and Gerard J. Gouw. 1990. "Athletic Footwear and Chronic Overloading." *Sports Medicine* 9(2): 76-85.

Robbins, S.E., and G.J. Gouw. 1991. "Athletic Footwear: Unsafe Due to Perceptual Illusions." *Medicine & Science in Sports & Exercise* 23(2): 217-224.

Robbins, S.E., E. Waked, P. Allard, J. McClaran, and N. Krouglicof. 1995. "Foot Position Awareness in Younger and Older Men: The Influence of Foot Wear Sole Properties." *Journal of the American Geriatrics Society* 45: 61–66.

Robbins, S.E., E. Waked, and J. McClaran. 1995. "Proprioception and Stability: Foot Position Awareness as a Function of Age and Footwear." *Age & Aging* 24: 67–72.

Robbins, Steven, and Edward Waked. 1997. "Hazard of Deceptive Advertising of Athletic Footwear." *British Journal of Sports Medicine* 31: 299-303.

Sekizawa, K., M.A. Sandrey, C. D. Ingersoll, and M.L. Cordova. 2001. "Effects of Shoe Sole Thickness on Joint Position Sense." *Gait & Posture* 13(3): 221–228.

[13] De Wit, B., D. De Clercq, and M. Lenoir. 1995. "The Effect of Varying Midsole Hardness on Impact Forces and Foot Motion during Foot Contact in Running." *Journal of Applied Biomechanics* 11(4): 394-406.

Dixon, S. J., A. C. Collop, and M. E. Batt. 2000. "Surface Effects on Ground Reaction Forces and Lower Extremity Kinematics in Running." *Medicine & Science in Sports & Exercise* 32(11): 1919-1926.

Hennig, E.M., A. Gordon, Q. Liu. 1996. "Biomechanical Variables and the Perception of Cushioning for Running in Various Types of Footwear." *Journal of Applied Biomechanics* 12(2): 143-150.

Milani, T. L., E. M. Hennig, and M. A. Lafortune. 1997. "Perceptual and Biomechanical Variables for Running in Identical Shoe Constructions with Varying Midsole Hardness." *Clinical Biomechanics* 12(5): 294-300.

Nigg, B. M., H. A. Bahlsen, S. M. Luethi, and S. Stokes. 1987. "The Influence of Running Velocity and Midsole Hardness on External Impact Forces in Heel-Toe Running." *Journal of Biomechanics* 20(10): 951-959.

Nigg, B. M., W. Herzog, and L. J. Read. 1988. "Effect of Viscoelastic Shoe Insoles on Vertical Impact Forces in Heel-Toe Running." *American Journal of Sports Medicine* 16(1): 70-76.

[14] Wallden, M. 2010. "Shifting Paradigms." *Journal of Bodywork & Movement Therapies* 14(2): 185-194.

Sarhmann, Shirley. 2002. *Diagnosis and Treatment of Movement Impairment Syndromes*. Saint Louis: Mosby.

[15] Lieberman, Daniel E., Madhusudhan Venkadesan, William A. Werbel, Adam I. Daoud, Susan D'Andrea, Irene S. Davis, Robert Ojiambo Mang'Eni, and Yannis Pitsiladis. 2010. "Foot Strike Patterns and Collision Forces in Habitually Barefoot versus Shod Runners." *Nature* 463: 531-536.

[16] McDougal, Christopher. 2011. *Born to Run: A Hidden Tribe, Superathletes, and the Greatest Race the World Has Never Seen*. New York: Vintage.

[17] Lieberman, Daniel E., Madhusudhan Venkadesan, William A. Werbel, Adam I. Daoud, Susan D'Andrea, Irene S. Davis, Robert Ojiambo Mang'Eni, and Yannis Pitsiladis. 2010. "Foot Strike Patterns and Collision Forces in Habitually Barefoot versus Shod Runners." *Nature* 463: 531-536, p.531.

[18] Robbins, Steven, and Edward Waked. 1997. "Hazard of Deceptive Advertising of Athletic Footwear." *British Journal of Sports Medicine* 31: 299-303.

[19] Hatala, K.G., H.L. Dingwall, R.E. Wunderlich, and B.G. Richmond. 2013. "Variation in Foot Strike Patterns during Running among Habitually Barefoot Populations." *PLoS One* 8(1): e52548. doi: 10.1371/journal.pone.0052548.

[20] McGee, Bobby. 2010. "Triathlon: The Run." *USA Triathlon Training DVD Series.*

[21] D'Aout, K.; T.C. Pataky; D. De clercq; and P. Aerts. "The Effects of Habitual Footwear Use: Foot Shape and Function in Native Barefoot Walkers." *Footwear Science* 1(2): 81-94.

[22] Jackson, R. 1990. "The Chinese Foot-binding Syndrome: Observations on the History and Sequelae of Wearing Ill-fitting Shoes." *International Journal of Dermatology* 29(5): 322-328.

[23] Dicharry, Jay. 2012. *Anatomy for Runners: Unlocking Your Athletic Potential for Health, Speed, and Injury Prevention.* New York: Skyhorse Publishing, p. 127.

[24] D'Aout, K.; T.C. Pataky; D. De clercq; and P. Aerts.

"The Effects of Habitual Footwear Use: Foot Shape and Function in Native Barefoot Walkers." *Footwear Science* 1(2): 81-94, p. 81.

[25] Robbins, Steven E., and Adel M. Hanna. 1987 . "Running-related Injury Prevention through Barefoot Adaptations." *Medicine & Science in Sports & Exercise* 19(2): 148-157.

[26] Frederick, E.C., J.T. Daniels, and J.W. Hayes. 1984. "The Effect of Shoe Weight on the Aerobic Demands of Running." In N. Bachl, L. Prokop, and R. Suckert (eds.) *Current Topics in Sports Medicine*, pgs. 616-625. Vienna: Urban & Schwarzenberg.

[27] Franz, Jason R., Corbyn M. Wierzbinski, and Rodger Kram. 2012. "Metabolic Cost of Running Barefoot versus Shod: Is Lighter Better?" *Medicine & Science in Sports & Exercise* 44(8): 1519-1525.

[28] Luckhaupt, Sara E. 2012. "Short Sleep Duration Among Workers." Centers for Disease Control and Prevention. Available: http://www.cdc.gov/mmwr/preview/mmwrhtml/mm61 16a2.htm?s_cid=mm6116a2_w.

ADAM HODGES

ABOUT THE AUTHOR

Adam Hodges, PhD, is a trail runner, multisport athlete, and coach with credentials from USA Triathlon, USA Cycling, and the American College of Sports Medicine. He has worked with high school cross country and track runners in California, masters swimmers in Colorado, and multisport athletes around the world. As a USAT All-American triathlete, he has competed in the ITU World Triathlon Championships, the ITU World Duathlon Championships, and the Ironman World Championships in Hawaii. As a masters runner, he has won a series championship in the XTERRA SoCal Trail Run Series. He began running in his youth and enjoys passing on the knowledge and experience he has gained over the years to both new and experienced runners seeking to maximize enjoyment, competitiveness, and longevity in the sport.

27024016R00100

Made in the USA
Lexington, KY
24 October 2013